ILLUSTRATOR:
ANDREA TSURUMI

WRITING PARTNER:
SARAH HUTT

TECHNICAL ADVISOR:
JEFF STERN

EDITOR:
KENDRA LEVIN

ART DIRECTOR:
KATE RENNER

RESHMA SAUJANI

girls who **code**

LEARN to CODE and CHANGE the WORLD

Virgin BOOKS

1 3 5 7 9 10 8 6 4 2

Virgin Books, an imprint of Ebury Publishing,
20 Vauxhall Bridge Road,
London SW1V 2SA

Virgin Books is part of the Penguin Random House group of companies whose addresses
can be found at global.penguinrandomhouse.com

Penguin
Random House
UK

First published in the United Kingdom by Virgin Books in 2017
First published in the United States by Viking in 2017

www.penguin.co.uk

A CIP catalogue record for this book is available from the British Library
ISBN: 9780753557600

Printed and bound in Slovakia by TBB, a.s.

Penguin Random House is committed to a sustainable future for our business,
our readers and our planet. This book is made from Forest Stewardship Council ® certified
paper.

MIX
Paper from
responsible sources
FSC
www.fsc.org   FSC® C018179

This book is dedicated
to all the girls who code
and to the girls who
will one day.

CONTENTS

OUR GIRLS WHO CODE

Lucy

BIRTHDAY: May 20th
LIKES: science, music, video games, emojis, trying new things

Sophia

BIRTHDAY: November 13th
LIKES: sports, sweatpants, babysitting, nail art, taking selfies

Maya

BIRTHDAY: June 3rd
LIKES: writing, drawing, fashion, chunky jewelry, giving advice

Erin

BIRTHDAY: February 26th
LIKES: baking, theater, reading, surfing, doing silly impressions

Leila

BIRTHDAY: August 22nd
LIKES: robotics, gardening, field hockey, crafting, hanging out with her big sister

HELLO, WORLD

I'M RESHMA, and I'm the founder of Girls Who Code.

Our organization helps girls in middle school and beyond learn to write code that's used to program computers and digital devices and get inspired by all the amazing ideas, skills, and opportunities that learning to code can bring.

And, believe me, there are tons.

But I'll let you in on a little secret: UNTIL A FEW YEARS AGO, I WAS AFRAID TO LEARN HOW TO CODE.

My background is as a lawyer and politician. I've served as the deputy public advocate for New York City, and in 2010, I was the first South Asian

American woman to run for Congress. I've always loved meeting new people and helping out in my community. That's why I was drawn to politics. Ever since I was a girl, I've aspired to do something that would make a positive difference in people's lives. I just never imagined it would be through computers or coding.

But when I was running for office, I spent a lot of time visiting New York City schools. That's when I noticed something.

In every computer lab, I saw dozens of boys learning to code and training to be tech innovators. BUT THERE WERE BARELY ANY GIRLS!

Where were they?

This didn't seem right to me. I knew that women make up a majority of college graduates and almost half our workforce. But when it came to computer science, or CS, the study of computers and the different ways they can be used, women weren't anywhere to be seen (at least in New York City's schools). And that's a problem.

By 2020, there will be 1.4 million open jobs in computing. These jobs are some of the country's highest-paying and fastest-growing career paths. BUT GIRLS ARE ON TRACK TO FILL JUST 4 PERCENT OF THEM.

Just 4 percent? If this were a pie chart, that wouldn't even qualify as a slice!

To me, this is unacceptable. Girls are missing out on the jobs of the future, all because they are not learning to code.

Why is this happening? Why weren't there more girls in those classrooms?

THE PROBLEM

It got me thinking about why *I'd* never learned to code.

It wasn't because I didn't have plenty of opportunities to study math and computing; after all, my dad is an engineer. When I was growing up, he loved to share science ideas with me and would always ask me math questions on the fly, usually during dinner. But it was hard for me to work out the answers in my head. A lot of times I knew the answer, but I couldn't figure it out right away. And those moments of not knowing and staring at my dad's face across the table made me feel like I wasn't smart enough. Dinner became an anxiety-filled event for me, and I started to believe I wasn't good at math.

Then I became scared of it.

So I avoided it, and any subject I thought required math—including coding, statistics, and engineering—and focused on history and writing, where I was more comfortable and knew I would do well immediately.

I didn't realize it at the time, but I wasn't alone. Thousands of girls of all ages tell me the same thing: that they're just "not good" at math or science. They tell me they're scared of subjects that seem too technical, like coding. Or even if they're not scared, they think computer science is not "for" them—that it's not social enough, and it's for boys who like to sit at computers all day.

Well, let me tell you another secret:

THAT IS COMPLETE AND UTTER BALONEY ON A ROLL! (*hold the mayo*)

It turns out that from an early age, we've been fed the message through stereotypes, social cues, and sometimes even from educators that science, technology, engineering, and math, or STEM, is "not for you."

If you start looking for these signals, you'll see them everywhere. I can walk into a popular retailer for teen girls and buy a T-shirt that says ALLERGIC TO ALGEBRA. Or I can watch any number of TV shows depicting a programmer as a guy in a hoodie alone with his computer in his basement.

As girls, we're listening. And you can see the impact of these negative stereotypes and lack of role models in the numbers. By middle school, most girls say that STEM careers are not for them. By high school, girls are ranking engineering, computing, and math as some of the least interesting professions.

Girls are being slowly steered away from STEM subjects before they can find out if they actually like them, and, more importantly, before they can find out that they are actually *amazing* at them.

THE NEXT STEP

In 2010, I lost my race for Congress. That was hard for me. As a lifelong high achiever, I had never failed at anything before, and it took me a while to figure out what to do next. But it also made me realize something that changed my life: my decision to run for Congress took a lot of courage. I had to be brave, and even though I failed, I knew that I had tried. I'd reached outside my comfort zone and done something new, something different, something scary. It made me wonder if, had I done that all those years ago at the dinner table or in school, I might have discovered that I loved coding or math or science.

That's when I knew it was time to be brave again and use what I'd learned to try to change the game for the next generation of young women.

I decided I was going to teach girls to code. It was an experiment, and I started with a classroom of twenty girls in New York City. I convinced a friend to lend me a conference room at his company and went door-to-door to recruit the first students. I had no idea how people would respond, but I knew I had to try.

TODAY, GIRLS WHO CODE HAS BUILT A MOVEMENT. We run one hundred summer programs and thousands of after-school clubs for middle- and high-school girls. We've reached tens of thousands of girls in every state in the country.

GUESS WHAT?

It turns out, girls are really good at coding!

They can build incredible things!

And they have fun doing it!

In this book, you'll read about some of my favorite creations made by real girls: from a game to help young girls see themselves as beautiful to a lighting system that can sense the beat in music and create light displays to match. When you learn to code, you give yourself a tool, a tech superpower, to create change in your community. You use *your* voice, *your* mind, and *your* skills to find solutions to problems to help your country. And you start to build a better world for each and every one of us.

Not to mention you can make great friends and have an awesome time, too.

SO WHAT ARE YOU WAITING FOR?

This book will teach you how to be a girl who codes and how to build amazing things. You'll learn the same fundamentals of coding that we teach in our Girls Who Code classrooms. You'll get an introduction to projects and the fun of learning how to code through games, art and design, robots, website and mobile apps, and online security. We'll also introduce you to women and girls doing incredible and inspiring things with code. I bet you'll come away with a burning desire to start creating and join our movement of girls around the country and across the world.

READY TO BE BRAVE? LET'S DIVE IN!

1

WHY CODING?

WELCOME!

Yes, you! The one reading this book. So glad you made it.

What brings you to coding?

Maybe you're already into COMPUTER SCIENCE and want to learn how to do more.

If so, that's great!

Maybe a parent or grandparent or teacher told you that coding is a valuable skill for your future and made you sign up for a class, but you're not really sure if it's for you.

That's okay, too.

Maybe you don't know anything about coding and just liked our cover art.

That works for us!

Whatever the reason, we're glad you've picked up this book, and we're glad you're here. And you're in good company!

The first thing to know about coding is that it's about way more than just computers.

It's about having fun.

It's about collaborating with your friends.

It's something *everyone* (not just boys) can do.

And it's about creating, imagining, and inventing awesome new stuff based on whatever you're interested in.

REALLY? LIKE WHAT?

Like turning a toy car into a robot. Or making a WEBSITE* for your dog-walking business. Maybe you want to DESIGN a smart bracelet that can remind you when to do your home-work or practice the piano. Or an app to keep track of your sprint times when you're training. How about an interactive sound and light display for the next school play? Or an LED headband that can change color to match what you're wearing?

You can do all this stuff, and a whole lot more, by learning to code.

*When you see a word that looks like **THIS**, it means you can find a definition of it in the glossary on pages 158-162!

And I've got some news for you:

The major, earth-shattering trick to COMPUTER CODING is . . .

. . . it's mostly problem-solving!

The actual code-writing part is just a small piece of a process that uses the thinking and planning skills you already have and use every day in your life.

So let's get started.

First of all, who can tell me what coding is?

> OOOH, I KNOW THIS. IT'S HOW YOU TELL A COMPUTER WHAT TO DO.

That's right.

Coding is, very simply, writing commands to instruct a computer to do something in a programming language it can understand.

There are actually hundreds of different programming languages used to give instructions to a computer. Which one you use depends on what you need the computer to do. When you learn to code, you learn to "speak" one of these languages so that you can communicate directly to the computer.

> YEAH, BUT DON'T WE ALREADY TELL OUR COMPUTERS WHAT TO DO BY CLICKING ON THE MOUSE AND NAVIGATING DIFFERENT MENUS AND APPS? WHY DO I NEED TO KNOW CODING, TOO?

Because coding is an amazing tool that will allow you to use your computer in ways you haven't even dreamed up yet. Sure, you can already do stuff on your computer, your tablet, or your phone, but that's because at some point, somewhere, a programmer had an idea for that app or program, then wrote the CODE to make it work. That person's code created the icons and buttons and shortcuts you use to control your device. This is the software that runs the machine. But using software is not the same as writing code.

By learning to code, you no longer have to just use the programs and apps that somebody else created—you can build them yourself! Like a best friend birthday reminder app, or a website for your drama club.

SOFTWARE VS HARDWARE

SOFTWARE is the set of programs and applications that make a computer run. It's a collection of code, designed and written by programmers. Software includes everything from apps that let you put fun filters on your photos to games that let you take care of a virtual dog or fight villains. Software also includes the computer programs that let you write your English essay.

HARDWARE refers to the physical parts of the computer itself: the screen, the keyboard, the camera, and more. These are usually designed and built by engineers. Your phone and tablet are also examples of hardware.

Another great reason to learn to code: it helps you understand, design, and work with the technology of the future.

There's a computer in almost everything, including cars, games, medical devices, and clothes. There are even smart toothbrushes!

If an object doesn't rely on a computer right now, chances are good that, in a few years, it will. And every one of these digital devices depends on a programmer writing code to tell the machine what to do and how to do it.

THE NUMBER PI SQUARED IS 9.86960440109 . . .

SO WRITING CODE IS A REALLY IMPORTANT JOB?

Yes! Without a programmer writing code, a computer would just be a big box. Because even though today's computers can do amazing things, they are still machines that, at some level, need to be instructed by a person.

WHAT COMPUTERS DO

Think about the microwave in your kitchen. It won't just randomly start heating up your leftover mac and cheese because you want it to. You

have to put your dish in the microwave, close the door, set the timer, and push Start. The machine performs the task you instructed it to, and at the end, you pull out your warmed-up snack. The whole sequence happens because *you* decided you were hungry and programmed the machine to do what you wanted.

At a really basic level, a computer works the same way. You put something in, instruct the computer to do something with it, and you get the result.

The steps look like this:

$$\text{INPUT} \twoheadrightarrow \text{PROCESS} \twoheadrightarrow \text{OUTPUT}$$

There are a lot of ways to input information into computers. The most obvious way is with the tool used to write these words: the keyboard. A keyboard lets you input letters and numbers. The output is typed text, like this book you're reading. But a keyboard isn't the only way to get information into a computer. Digital pens, video cameras, microphones, scanners, and sensors also let you input information for your computer to interact with in tons of different ways.

And "information" doesn't always mean facts or figures. It can be music, video clips, brushstrokes, or photos. You can use software to edit your movies, manipulate a vocal track, fill in colors, add brightness and shadow, animate a game, drop filters onto a selfie, and upload it to your profile. You can do all this thanks to someone who had an idea for a program.

The program is what the computer will do with the information you've put in. It's basically the job you are asking the computer to do, or the PROCESS you are asking the computer to run on the data you have INPUT.

The OUTPUT is the result. An enhanced photo, a Word document, a calculation, an edited movie, an animation—it's what you get after the computer has run the program.

For every smart device or computer program you use daily, a programmer with an idea got together with other programmers and figured out exactly what they wanted the computer to be able to do. They thought about how the person using the computer would need to operate it. Then they designed the software, wrote the code to run it, tested it to be sure it worked, and *voilà*!

Thanks to some of those coders, you can cover your social media feeds in endless versions of awesome emojis.

When you learn to code, *you* will be able to do the same thing. And you might already have a ton of great ideas for useful and important programs that could change the world.

What do you think about that, emoji?

WOW, SO I COULD WRITE PROGRAMS THAT CAN MAKE A COMPUTER DO WHAT I WANT? LIKE MAKE MY OWN GAMES? OR APPS?

Yes! That's what coding is! You have the power to make computers work for you.

And as technology keeps evolving, having some coding superpowers will be important for helping you use the devices that will be developed next. The tech you'll be using by the time you're in college will probably be totally different from what you're using now.

> ARE THINGS REALLY CHANGING THAT FAST?

Yes. Take it from someone who used a landline phone attached to the kitchen wall to chat with her friends in middle school and whose playlists went onto mixtapes.

YOU MIGHT HAVE TO GOOGLE WHAT THESE THINGS ARE!

COMPUTERS, THEN AND NOW

To see how fast technology has evolved, let's take a look at where computers came from. You might be surprised to discover that some of computer science's most important thinkers and inventors were women you don't read much about in history books!

The earliest computers were used, as you may have guessed from the name, to compute stuff—mostly numbers. Calculating and tabulating devices have been around for thousands of years. They were used by early civilizations to keep track of large numbers, navigate their ships, and study the night skies. But it took many centuries of innovation before anything resembling a modern computer began to take shape.

The first fully mechanized computer that could take input in the form of num-

COMPUTER HISTORY PART I: THE FIRST COMPUTERS

Abacus: Invented by the Babylonians, this beaded calculating tool spread throughout the ancient world and into China.

3000 BC

Quipu: This Incan mathematical recording system used knotted string to represent numbers.

1400

YEAR ONE

35,000–20,000 BC

Lebombo and Ishango bones: Discovered in Africa, these notched baboon bones are the oldest known calculating tools.

AD 79

Antikythera mechanism: This was used in ancient Greece to calculate months and astronomical positions.

1622

Slide rule: Invented by William Oughtred, this device built on the theories of Scottish mathematician John Napier, who invented the logarithm, a system to speed up mathematical calculations. This device was used all the way until the invention of the electronic calculator, hundreds of years later!

bers, process a calculation, and then output a result was created in 1822 by a British mathematician and engineer named Charles Babbage. His "Difference Engine" was made of metal gears and levers. At that time most people doing large calculations for shipping, manufacturing, and banking relied on printed tables that were slow to sort through and often full of errors—not something you want when you are calculating the weight of a shipping container or a large financial transaction. Babbage's mechanical calculator was designed to solve this problem by being both fast and accurate.

Although the machine was never fully completed, the design was a breakthrough. Babbage used it to sketch out an even more advanced machine, the "Analytical Engine." The design for the Analytical Engine laid the groundwork for what would become the modern computer. It also showed the world the need for an instrument that could perform calculations quickly, precisely, and without human error.

Calculating clock: Built by German thinker Wilhelm Schickard, this was the first mechanical calculator. It could add and subtract six-digit numbers and was used to calculate astronomical tables.

1623

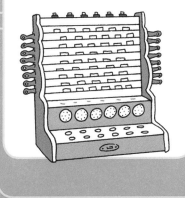

Punched-card system: Invented by Joseph-Marie Jacquard, this system allowed different machines like music boxes, player pianos, counters, and looms to be automated.

1801

Difference Engine: Designed and partially built by Charles Babbage, this machine was the predecessor to the modern computer.

1822

1674

Stepped reckoner: Invented by German philosopher Gottfried Wilhelm Leibniz, this device could add, subtract, and divide.

1820

Arithmometer: Invented by Charles Xavier Thomas, this was the first mass produced calculator.

The world's first computer programmer
ADA LOVELACE

Augusta "Ada" Byron Lovelace was the daughter of the renowned British romantic-era poet Lord Byron. But that's not why she's still famous today. She's considered the world's first programmer. Not only was she brilliant, she broke the mold for women of her era. At age twelve, Ada produced detailed blueprints for a steam-powered flying machine. At seventeen, she met Charles Babbage, who became her lifelong friend and mentor. In 1843, when she was twenty-seven, he asked her to publish a set of notes on his design for the Analytical Engine. In one of the notes describing how to use the machine, Lovelace included step-by-step operating instructions. Although no one realized it at the time, these instructions on how to "program" the engine to produce a calculation turned out to be the world's first computer program. Today a programming language used to control space satellites is called ADA in her honor.

ELECTRONIC COMPUTERS

It took another 124 years of inspiration, invention, trial, error, and technological breakthroughs before a team created an electronic computer that could do what Babbage had dreamed of so many years before. The Electronic Numerical Integrator and Computer, or ENIAC, was the first fully functioning general-use electronic computer that did not rely on any moving mechanical parts. (Phew, that's a mouthful!) J. Presper Eckert and John Mauchly at the University of Pennsylvania built it for the U.S. military during World War II. FUN FACT: Historians suspect that during the ten years it was in operation, the ENIAC performed more calculations

than mankind had in all of human history up to that point. Yeah, that's a whole lot of math.

WOMEN, THE REAL COMPUTERS

The invention of ENIAC was a breakthrough for computing, but what most people don't know is that a team of six women actually programmed it. For every series of calculations the computer produced, these highly skilled women had to manually input all of the DATA and program the operations by loading punched cards, setting switches, and connecting cables. This technology was uncharted territory, and these incredible women were inventing the process as they went. Like many great women throughout history, at the time they never received credit for their pioneering work.

So let's give them credit now! *Thank you* to:

Frances Bilas Spence (1922–2013)
Jean Jennings Bartik (1924–2011)
Marlyn Wescoff Meltzer (1922–2008)
Kathleen "Kay" McNulty Mauchly Antonelli (1921–2006)
Frances Elizabeth "Betty" Holberton (1917–2001)
Ruth Lichterman Teitelbaum (1924–1986)

WOW! IF IT TOOK SO MANY WOMEN TO PROGRAM ONE COMPUTER, THEY MUST HAVE BEEN THE ONLY ONES WHO COULD USE IT.

That's a good point. The fact that only highly trained programmers could use early computers revealed a problem. For computers to really be useful, they needed to be small enough to have in a home or business, and everyone needed to be able to talk to them.

MISSION TO THE MOON

In 1969, humans did something amazing. They traveled more than 230,000 miles through the vacuum of space and landed on the moon for the first time—and they did it with about as much computing power as a pocket calculator has! Regardless, the Apollo Guidance Computer built into NASA's lunar module was a huge breakthrough in computing technology. It was one of the smallest computers on (and off) the planet at the time. NASA and engineers from Massachusetts Institute of Technology (MIT) managed to take a computer the size of seven refrigerators and shrink it

COMPUTER HISTORY PART II: THE RISE OF PERSONAL COMPUTING

ENIAC: Widely believed to be the grandfather of digital computers, this machine filled a twenty-by-forty-foot room and had **18,000** vacuum tubes.

1943–1944

COBOL programming language: This was the first English-like computer programming language; it eventually evolved into FORTRAN.

1953

Apollo Guidance Computers: These machines sent computing to the moon.

Unix: This operating system was developed at Bell Labs.

1969

1947

Transistor: Scientists at Bell Telephone Laboratories invented the transistor. This allowed them to make smaller electronic circuits and paved the way for personal computers.

1975

IBM 5100: This was the first modern desktop model computer with a keyboard, display monitor, and built-in storage.

Microsoft: Bill Gates and Paul Allen founded the company.

into a machine that weighed only seventy pounds and was roughly the size of a microwave. More important, it was equipped with software that allowed astronauts to type in commands using simple combinations of nouns and verbs, without the need for a programmer. With this computer, a user could control the machine without knowing how to code.

Apple computer: Steve Jobs and Steve Wozniak founded the company and sold their first computers, the Apple 1.

1976

1977

Apple II: This computer was released, bringing affordable mass-produced computers to mainstream consumers.

IBM Personal Computer: IBM released this computer, which runs on Microsoft's DOS operating system.

1981

1985

Windows: Microsoft released this new operating system.

America Online was founded.

The World Wide Web is invented.

1990

1988

First foldable laptop: This device was released by Compaq.

*One small step for man,
one giant leap for womankind!*

MARGARET HAMILTON

Did you know that a female mathematician, Margaret Hamilton, created the software for the Apollo program's two portable computers? She also coined the term "software engineering" while she was inventing the job! When the United States embarked on the Apollo lunar project in the 1960s, the field of computer science didn't really exist. Neither did the software to run the ship's onboard computers. Hamilton and her colleagues from MIT invented it. Their work was essential to safely landing the first humans on the moon, and it laid the groundwork for what would become a $4 billion worldwide industry.

COMPUTER HISTORY PART III: THE DAWN OF THE INTERNET

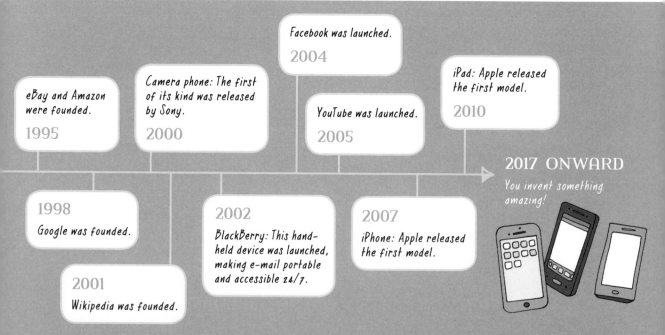

Facebook was launched.
2004

iPad: Apple released the first model.
2010

eBay and Amazon were founded.
1995

Camera phone: The first of its kind was released by Sony.
2000

YouTube was launched.
2005

2017 ONWARD
You invent something amazing!

1998
Google was founded.

2002
BlackBerry: This hand-held device was launched, making e-mail portable and accessible 24/7.

2007
iPhone: Apple released the first model.

2001
Wikipedia was founded.

WHERE WE ARE TODAY

Less than a decade after we landed on the moon, the first affordable, mass-produced personal computers brought computing power into the hands of everyday consumers. Constant breakthroughs in computer engineering and technology have continued to make these machines smaller and faster. With wireless and mobile technology, we've come to the world you know, where you can video chat with someone halfway around the world in real time from a device that fits into your pocket.

> I NEVER THOUGHT ABOUT COMPUTERS THIS WAY. IT'S KIND OF COOL TO THINK THAT BY CODING WE COULD BE INVENTORS AND PIONEERS.

> *I KNOW, RIGHT?* I'M READY TO LEARN HOW TO CODE. HOW DO WE GET STARTED?

There are a couple of ways to get started with coding. The first is to pick a programming language and dive right in with tutorials and practice. Another way is to explore how computers work, so you'll know what you can ask them to do and how to do the asking. That's what we're going to do here.

And I'll give you a tip: computers are smart, but they're not great at making sandwiches.

HOW TO TALK TO YOUR COMPUTER

EVEN THOUGH COMPUTERS ARE OFTEN REFERRED TO AS "THINKING machines" or "electronic brains," they actually need a lot of help. They're great at following instructions, but they can't always think for themselves. Which means that when you ask a computer to do something, your instructions have to be extremely precise.

This is because a computer will do *exactly* what you tell it to.

THE PEANUT BUTTER AND JELLY EFFECT

Imagine you get home from school and you see your very own robot standing in your kitchen, waiting for your orders. Cool, right? You're hungry, so you ask your robot—let's call it AwesomeBot 3000, aka Bot—to make you a peanut butter and jelly sandwich.

"I REQUIRE FURTHER INSTRUCTIONS," Bot says in its electronic robot-y voice. Everything for your sandwich is laid out on the kitchen counter, so you say, "OK, go to the counter, get the bread, put the peanut butter and jelly on the bread, and bring it to me."

So Bot rolls to the counter (did I mention it has wheels?), picks up the jar of peanut butter, picks up the jar of jelly, and puts them both on top of the bag of bread.

Computers are *super literal*. If you want Bot to make you a sandwich you can actually eat, you'd have to say something like this:

"Locate bread, open bag. Remove two pieces. Lay pieces flat on countertop, side by side. Roll two feet to right. Locate drawer. Open drawer, remove knife from drawer. Close drawer. Roll two feet to left. Locate peanut butter. Open jar. Insert knife into peanut butter . . ."

You get the idea.

To start coding, you have to know a programming language, but just as important, you have to understand how a computer thinks, so you can give it the right kinds of instructions to get it to do what you want.

HMMM! THAT SEEMS KIND OF TRICKY.

Actually, it's not, once you get the hang of COMPUTATIONAL THINKING—which basically means planning, problem solving, and analyzing information the way a computer does. Once you understand how computers process information, you will understand what they can and can't do. Knowing that will make coding much easier.

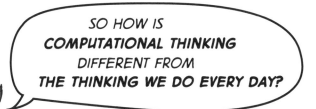

SO HOW IS **COMPUTATIONAL THINKING** DIFFERENT FROM **THE THINKING WE DO EVERY DAY?**

We use our brains to do a lot of sophisticated tasks with the information we take in from the world around us, like imagining or coming up with new ideas to solve problems or communicating thoughts and feelings to others using words and body language. These are the acts that computers can't quite do yet.

But computers are excellent at performing some of our most essential mental tasks.

The first one is *remembering* stuff. Computers remember every piece

of information you give them and, with the right program, how to find it. You can probably remember lots of things—like your best friend's birthday or how to get to your favorite ice cream place, but a computer can store billions and billions of facts, figures, numbers, photos, videos, games, and books.

Right now engineers are working on a supercomputer with enough memory to store the equivalent of 227,000 miles of stacked books.

That's enough books to cross the United States more than sixty-five times!

The second activity computers do really well is *repeat* stuff. We repeat things all the time; in fact, repetition—doing things over and over deliberately in the form of practice—is a big part of how we learn, like when you study for a test or memorize your lines for a show. Computers don't learn from repetition in the same way that we do, but they happen to be really good at it. They can repeat a calculation or task hundreds of times without ever getting tired, bored, or making a mistake. Think about how your phone wakes you up first thing in the morning, with its tinkling tones telling you it's time to start the day. When that alarm rings at the same time each school day, that's a computer program on your phone repeating itself . . . even if you wish it wouldn't.

Another job computers are good at is *deciding* things. These are not the major life decisions people make, like "What is my career going to be?" or "Should I tell my crush how I feel?" They are more like "Up or down? On or off? Chocolate or vanilla?" kinds of decisions. But these simple decisions, when structured the right way, are an important part of almost every computer program.

Think of a GPS in a car or on a phone. When you enter the address for where you want to go, the GPS's program looks at lots of information about the available routes, then decides to send you left or right, on this road or that one.

These tasks—remembering, repeating, making simple decisions—are the foundations of computational thinking. And if you put enough of them together . . .

GIRL, YOU'RE CODING!

But you can't just ask a computer to do these jobs in any order. You have to put these tasks together in a way the computer will understand. You have to follow certain rules.

Don't Forget How Computers Work

INPUT ≫ PROCESS ≫ OUTPUT

You already know coding is writing instructions for a computer in a programming language. And as with any language—English, French, Swahili, Hindi—there are rules we all have to follow so everyone can understand what we're saying. You can't just put words into random order and ex-

DATA is any information you put into a computer and use to perform a task or make a calculation.

LOGIC is the rules you want the computer to follow when it processes the data.

pect to be understood. Wise other, read like this you would, and like Yoda sound would we.

It's the same with coding. In fact, programming languages are even more specific and exact than spoken languages. Which is why even though different programming languages write code in their own ways, they all use a few of the same basic pieces. These pieces have to be laid out with a clear set of rules to describe the jobs they want the computer to do in a way it can understand.

Let's take a look at how we tell a computer to remember, repeat, or decide something in code.

VARIABLE = REMEMBER

When you are coding, specific information that you want the computer to remember is called a VARIABLE. A variable is like a container you can use to store information.

Are you into scrapbooking, sewing, painting, collage, or hairstyling?

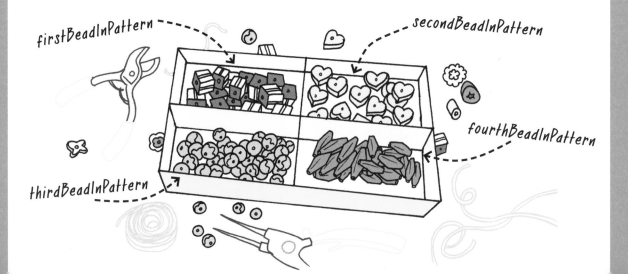

Variables are like craft boxes that you can keep different supplies and materials in. In real life you would label each box to tell you what goes inside—buttons, beads, crayons, hair ties. That way you can find what you need quickly. Naming your variables does the same thing—it creates a labeled container where you can keep information. The contents might change, but the labeled boxes stay the same. In coding, you use variables to identify and store all different kinds of changing data.

Variables can hold numbers, short sentences and sequences of numbers called STRINGS, or even true/false statements, known as BOOLEANS.

Here are some of the kinds of information you can store inside variables:

```
variableName = value;
```

Numbers: Variables can contain number data.

```
currentAge =12;                    daysLeftOfSchool = 234;
costOfIceCream = 2.50;             stringLengthInches = 7;
```

Text: Variables can hold long strings of text. The text is always surrounded by quotes.

```
mentorsName = "Leila";
favoriteSong = "Don't Stop Believin'";
dayOfTheWeek = "Friday";
statusUpdate = "I'm so excited that I'm learning to code!!";
```

Boolean: Variables can be used to hold True or False values. These are useful when it comes time to make a decision.

```
isWeekend = true;                  brotherIsAwake = false;
loggedIn = true;                   stillHaveString = true;
```

LOOP = REPEAT

A LOOP is a piece of code that tells the computer to repeat something. Just like your alarm clock repeats itself at the same time every day, loops are structures that repeat a process in the code.

Say you've got beads in one of your boxes and you are making a necklace. You want to put the beads in a certain pattern: ■♥●♦ and then repeat: ■♥●♦. Repeating the same pattern over and over again is your loop. When you create a loop in code, you have to also tell the computer under what

```
while(stillHaveBeads == true) {
    addBeadsToString();
}
```

STEP 1: THINK UP A PATTERN.

STEP 2: REPEAT PATTERN UNTIL OUT OF BEADS.

STEP 3: TIE OFF THE END WITH A CLASP.

conditions it should end or how many times it should repeat. Sometimes you'll create a loop that never ends, and this is called an infinite loop. In this example that would mean the world's longest necklace!

CONDITIONAL = DECIDE

CONDITIONALS are used when you need the computer to decide something. You probably deal with conditionals all the time. Maybe you've heard your parents or grandparents say something like, "You can watch a movie on the condition that you do all your homework first." So a condition is like the terms for doing or deciding something.

In coding we usually set conditions using an "if" statement. We use these kinds of statements to make decisions in our own lives all the time. *If* it is raining when I get ready to leave my house, then I put on my rain boots. *If* I'm hungry when I get home from school, then I have a snack. Now you try: think of a conditional you encounter in your daily life:

IF _____ , THEN _____ .

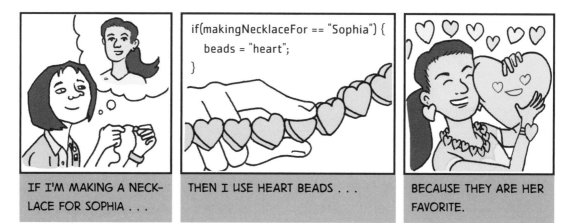

IF I'M MAKING A NECK-LACE FOR SOPHIA . . .

```
if(makingNecklaceFor == "Sophia") {
    beads = "heart";
}
```

THEN I USE HEART BEADS . . .

BECAUSE THEY ARE HER FAVORITE.

Sometimes you want something to happen only if the condition is *not* true. Then you would use an "else" statement to say what happens. *If* it is raining when I get ready to leave my house, then I put on my rain boots. *Else* (or "otherwise"), I wear sneakers. *If* I am hungry when I get home

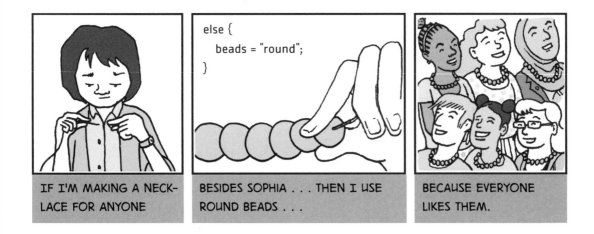

IF I'M MAKING A NECK-LACE FOR ANYONE

```
else {
    beads = "round";
}
```

BESIDES SOPHIA . . . THEN I USE ROUND BEADS . . .

BECAUSE EVERYONE LIKES THEM.

from school, I eat a snack; *else* I start my homework right away. If and/or else set up the conditions.

UHH . . .

HOW DOES ALL THIS HELP ME UNDERSTAND HOW TO CODE?

Variables, loops, and conditionals are some of the most basic building blocks you can use to start writing codes that can tell your computer what to do. These are the pieces you need to start coding a video game or a social media site. In fact, they're so important that, along with functions (which you'll discover in the next chapter), we call them the CORE4 computer science concepts. Once you understand these pieces,

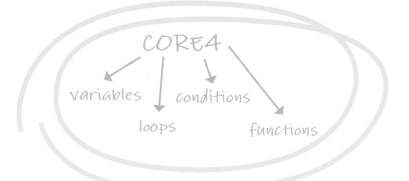

CORE4
variables | conditions
loops
functions

you can use them to outline the real-life situations you want to reproduce in your coding project, following rules the computer can understand.

And just like that, you can start creating.

REMEMBERING, REPEATING, AND DECIDING ARE REALLY ALL IT TAKES TO MAKE MY E-MAIL OR THE GAMES ON MY PHONE WORK?

Well, it's a little more complicated than that, but these tasks are the fundamentals of a lot of code, including code that runs big software like Wikipedia, Instagram, and WhatsApp. We're going to tell you how in the next chapter. And there will be tacos involved.

P.S. Why did the chicken keep crossing the road?

Because she was programmed on an infinite loop!

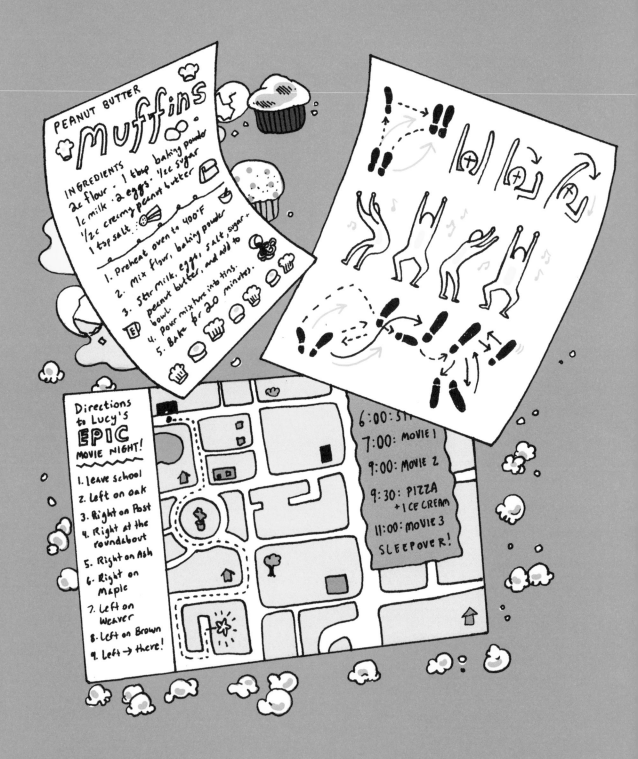

3

PUTTING IT ALL TOGETHER

IF YOU'VE HEARD ANYTHING ABOUT CODING BEFORE PICKING UP this book, then you might recognize the word ALGORITHMS. This big, mysterious-sounding word seems to be the magic formula that makes your Internet searches work and your online shopping preferences pop up. But algorithms aren't just for computer scientists. You actually deal with them every single day, many times a day, and probably don't even realize it.

An algorithm is simply a set of instructions you follow in a certain order to complete a task.

A muffin recipe is an algorithm. So is a dance routine, or directions to a friend's house. Even something as basic as your morning routine can be an algorithm.

It probably goes something like this: wake up, get out of bed, brush teeth, pick out clothes, put on clothes . . . all the way to put on shoes and jacket and walk out the door.

You follow this algorithm almost every day to get the same result: you, dressed and on your way to school.

Getting ready in the morning seems simple—so simple you can do it while half-asleep! But it actually involves a lot of very detailed steps.

Just putting on your socks and shoes and tying the laces is a multi-step process.

Remember our robot friend, Bot, from the last chapter? Bot showed us that the algorithm for making a peanut butter and jelly sandwich is actually pretty complicated when you break it down. But algorithms serve as clear road maps that anyone, even *super literal* robots, can follow.

> SO WHEN I DO MY WARM-UPS BEFORE TRACK PRACTICE, OR PUT ON SHOES, OR WASH MY HAIR, *I'VE BEEN USING ALGORITHMS ALL THIS TIME?*

Yes, and that's not all. You also use some of the most detailed coding algorithms in the world every day. When you do a Google search, look up a local weather forecast on your phone, or consider the "just-for-you" recommendations on your streaming video services like YouTube or Netflix or on online shopping sites, all that information is found and delivered to you by complex algorithms designed and coded by programmers.

If you liked My Neighbor Totoro, you might like:

SPIRITED AWAY

AVATAR
THE LAST AIRBENDER

Coraline

> SO A PROGRAM IS KIND OF LIKE A BIG ALGORITHM WRITTEN IN A WAY A COMPUTER CAN UNDERSTAND.

You are 100 percent correct. The algorithm in a program is the set of instructions you want the computer to follow. This is *not* the actual code; it's steps in a task that you will *turn into* code.

You already know that computers are really good at certain tasks like remembering, repeating, and making simple decisions. An algorithm puts these different jobs together into a sequence the computer can follow to deliver a result. This is what you end up coding, in whatever programming language works best for the job.

Why don't we come up with an example of something you do every day that we can write out as an algorithm and use it to identify variables, conditionals, and loops?

Any ideas?

> HOW ABOUT PICKING WHAT TO EAT FOR LUNCH?

Perfect. We'll call it the Lunch Line Algorithm. Leila, you're at the board.

This is just one small algorithm, but if you wanted to, you could create one for each of you, for the whole school year, using all different kinds of foods. Regardless of how big or complicated your algorithm is, the basic steps remain the same.

Let's see what the Lunch Line Algorithm might look like in pseudocode. PSEUDOCODE uses normal everyday writing to spell out exactly what you will be coding as very precise instructions.

```
if Lucy orders tacos:
    while there are tacos left to fill:
        Lunch server fills tacos
else:
    Lunch server serves pizza

Lunch server serves Lucy apple juice
and bananas
```

I CAN READ THAT. I MEAN, *IT MAKES SENSE!* I CAN SEE WHAT EACH STEP IS.

That's the beauty of pesudocode—it's a method of planning your code in English first so then you can translate it into computer code. Let's look at how we would do that.

D.R.Y.

You'll see that there are a few elements of the pseudocode that repeat, like the filling for the taco, which is always chicken and guacamole. Repeated code happens a lot when you are writing a program because you often need to ask the program to do the same thing over and over.

But you don't need to write those lines again and again! There's a saying many programmers learn early on: "DRY." Not "dry" like what you do to your hair after swim class—D.R.Y.: Don't Repeat Yourself. Two key ingredients to writing good algorithms and good code are clarity, which you already know from our robot friend, Bot, and efficiency. Keep your code simple, clear, and streamlined. Luckily there are a few shortcuts that can help you do just that.

LUNCH LINE, LOOPS

Let's say it's Taco Tuesday—yippee! Since every time Lucy eats tacos she gets the same filling, the instruction in the algorithm, and therefore the code, will always be the same: fill all three tacos with chicken and guacamole. In code, that pattern might look like this:

```
taco1.fill("chicken")

taco1.fill("guacamole")

taco2.fill("chicken")

taco2.fill("guacamole")
```

```
taco3.fill("chicken")

taco3.fill("guacamole")
```

Wow, that's a lot of code and typing! Instead of writing this code over and over again for all of Lucy's tacos, you can write a loop to repeat it for you.

```
for each taco in lucysOrder:

    taco.fill ("chicken")

    taco.fill ("guacamole")
```

Now all three of your tacos will be filled the same way, and our code is only three lines. But what if we wanted to use different fillings for each taco? Let's take a look at functions!

FUNCTIONS

Functions, the fourth member of the Core4 concepts along with variables, loops, and conditionals, are little bunches of code that do specific jobs in a larger program. You can create them for lots of reasons, but a big one is to help you avoid having to write the same code over and over again. All you have to do is write a function and name it, and then any time you want to use it, you call it up in your code by typing in its name, and it will run your bunch of code in that part of your program. It's like creating a button or a shortcut to automatically do a job in your code without your needing to write out the instructions every time.

I WISH I HAD ONE FOR PUTTING MY LAUNDRY AWAY!

I'm sure somebody out there is working on a laundry-folding robot. But in the meantime, let's go back to our Lunch Line Algorithm and take a look at how a function can work in a program.

DEFINING YOUR FUNCTION

The first step to making any function is to define it. Give it a name—otherwise your program won't know how to find that batch of code when it's time to use it. Names should be clear and descriptive. So, in this case, let's name our function the **fill_my_taco** function!

Once you've named it, you have to write the code for it. Part of doing that means creating PARAMETERS in your function. Parameters are like little mini variables inside a function. They hold information that may change.

In code it would look like this:

```
def fill_my_taco(taco, item1, item2):

    taco.fill(item1)

    taco.fill(item2)
```

The parameters are the content in parentheses. In this **fill_my_taco** function we can fill our taco with two different items.

CALLING ALL FUNCTIONS

Once you have your function built, all you have to do is actually use it in the code. This is an important step. It's not enough just to define and build a function; you have to tell the computer when and where you want to use it. You do that by typing the function name in the part of the code where you want it to run. This is known as "calling" the function.

Calling the function in the code would look like this:

```
fill_my_taco(taco1, "chicken", "guacamole")
```

And we can try using different fillings for our other tacos as well!

```
fill_my_taco(taco2, "tofu", "salsa")
```

```
fill_my_taco(taco3, "beans", "vegetables")
```

Now we have three different tacos. Mmmmm . . . variety!

Functions can also be represented as buttons or shortcuts on the user side of a program, like the print button in a word processing app or the back button on a web browser. Click any one of those buttons when you are using that program, and it will call up the function in the code and activate it.

LIBRARIES

Functions are huge time-savers when you really start coding. And they aren't the only shortcut in coding. Libraries are also an important resource for coders. We're not talking about your local library, where you go to check out books. (Yay, we 💜 libraries!) Code libraries store useful algorithms and pieces of code that someone has already written so that others can use them in their programs. These libraries let programmers access all kinds of handy code:

★ Algorithms for searching, like the kind that power Google or Microsoft's search engine.

★ Algorithms for sorting that help you categorize data different ways—alphabetically, by number, by name, etc.

★ Recommendation algorithms, which take input or search patterns and use them to make suggestions for a certain user, just like the "movies for you" on Netflix or products on Amazon.

Not only does using ready-made code like functions and libraries save programmers a lot of time and energy, it also helps you share your beautiful, precise, and efficient pieces of code with the community.

APIs

APIs or application programming interfaces are another helpful tool in coding. APIs are a way for one APPLICATION to share information with another application. Today, *lots* of applications have APIs for anyone to use: Yelp, National Weather Service, Google Maps, Pinterest, and Twitter, to name a few. You can use code from these and other companies in your own program to let you embed tweets on a web page or display weather information about a person's current location. APIs create a little doorway into a program's code so other programs can share data or services, and they are a great example of how computer programmers are working together to make great technology.

Here's a super fun mobile app three girls in our GWC community created using algorithms, APIs, and functions.

Forecast Fabulous
Where are you heading?

48203

Submit

Faboo 'Dos for You

This handy app makes sure you always have the right hairdo for the right weather. It was created by Kenisha J., Serena V., and Faith W.

Here's how they describe the idea for the app:

"We've noticed that a common problem amongst women is that we don't *all* just wake up with our hair looking perfect. We have to take into

account a variety of different environmental factors such as the weather and the humidity when getting ready. The result? Much needed time is inadvertently wasted while we look for new and easy hairstyles to match the conditions. To solve this problem, we have come up with Forecast Fabulous.

"Forecast Fabulous is a mobile application that allows users to input their hair length, hair type, and the zip code of where they are going, and it generates a hairstyle for them based on the information. As a result, women no longer have to worry about the weather 'cramping their style.' Looking fabulous will never be a problem again with Forecast Fabulous!"

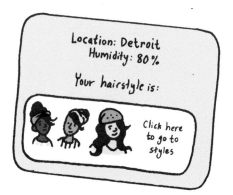

Here's a peek inside some of the Javascript code that makes this app run. Don't worry—you don't have to understand this perfectly. We've highlighted some key parts.

```
var zip = document.getElementById("usersZip").value;

$.ajax({

    url: "https://api.wunderground.com/
    api/2f800aa485a60839/geolookup/
    conditions/q/" + zip + ".json",

    dataType: "jsonp",
```

This line checks what the user typed in for her local zip code and saves it to a VARIABLE called "zip" (as in "zip code").

This uses the zip code to retrieve the latest weather data for that area from the API of a website called Weather Underground.

```
                    success : function(weatherData) {

          var location = weatherData['location']['city'];

          var temp_f = weatherData['current_observation']
          ['temp_f'];

       }

    });


    alert("Current temperature in " + location + " is: " + temp_f);
```

If the API works, this brings the information about the weather in this zip code from Weather Underground and stores it.

This code allowed the girls to save just the name of their city from the weather data to a variable called "location."

This code is where the girls save just the temperature information from the weather data to a variable called "temp_f" (for Fahrenheit!).

Here the girls use the information they collected to tell the user what the current temperature is with the city name.

These girls made this app by taking variables and putting them to-gether as a handy-dandy algorithm. They coded it, adding functions and using an API to provide weather data. And, *presto*! An app to keep you sleek, styling, and frizz-free no matter the weather!

So *if* . . .

you are ready to start building, *then* take a peek at our next chapter, which is all about getting started.

If you are not sure what you want to build, *then* you might want to jump to Chapter 7 to see examples for some inspiration for the many things that you can build with programming!

But first let's find out which animal is more like you: a puppy or a kitten.

GETTING STARTED

WHO'S READY TO GET STARTED ON A PROJECT?

What are you going to build? How are you going to do it? What's the plan?

If those questions make you feel like a deer in the headlights, don't worry—you're not alone. Getting started can be the toughest part of any project. But it can also be the most exciting and creative. And there are lots of different ways to dive in.

TAKE IT FROM THE TOP

When it comes to getting started on a new project, any new project, every-one's reaction is unique. But it usually ranges somewhere between two ends of a spectrum we'll call "The Puppy at the Park" and "The Kitten with a Toy."

The Puppy at the Park is some-one who loves a new project. These people have no hesitation getting started. They love coming up with ideas. They are brimming with inspi-ration and excitement and want to chase down every idea that pops into their heads. This kind of energy is fan-tastic, but sometimes these starters can get lost chasing the butterflies of new ideas and wear themselves out before they're done with a project.

Kittens with a Toy do the opposite when it comes to starting some-thing new. They often seem like they are just not that interested. In fact, sometimes this type of starter feels a little overwhelmed by the thought of a new project. But what they are really doing is sizing it up, thinking, planning, and looking for a way to get going. And once these kittens pounce, they have tons of fun.

In an ideal world, everyone would land somewhere in the middle—where you aren't scared to get started, but you also take time to consider what you want to do and plan it out thoughtfully.

The good news is that no matter what kind of starter you are, and no matter how big the project you're starting is, there is a tried and true method for taking the first step.

Anyone want to take a guess what it is?

The best way to start any big job is to break it down into smaller, more doable tasks. This gives you a clear path to follow and helps you keep from feeling totally overwhelmed.

So let's look at a few ways to do this with a coding project.

THE DESIGN-BUILD-TEST CYCLE

In coding, and in a lot of product development, designers and programmers work through something called the "design-build-test cycle." It looks like this.

You start by designing your product, then you build it, then you test it to make sure it's doing what you want it to. Often, testing will lead you back to designing as

you identify problem areas that aren't working or places that could be improved.

BUT WHAT IF YOU DON'T KNOW WHAT TO DESIGN?

There's a process for that, too. It's usually the very first step in coding, and for a lot of people, it's the most fun part!

CLOUDY WITH A CHANCE OF BRAINSTORMS

Before you ever write a single line of code, you have to figure out what problem you are trying to solve and what product will help you do that. Maybe there's an idea you've been kicking around for a while, a product you wish you had. Maybe it's something you already use and wish worked better. Maybe you don't have any ideas for projects at all, but you have a feeling about a style or look for something. Maybe you're interested in a play, a poem, a piece of music, a social cause, a sport, or even a favorite shade of blue. These are all great places to start your BRAINSTORMING— the process of using free, no-rules thinking to come up with ideas that you can build upon.

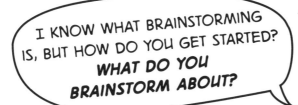

I KNOW WHAT BRAINSTORMING IS, BUT HOW DO YOU GET STARTED? **WHAT DO YOU BRAINSTORM ABOUT?**

One way is to start by thinking about topics that interest you. Propose a variety of scenarios, like: "When I'm timing my sprints on the track field, I wish I had a _____." or "When I'm researching endangered animals, I really want to know about _____." How about "When I'm looking for cake decoration ideas online, wouldn't it be great if I could _____?" Or "If I could have any app in the world, it would do _____." Or "I use this device every day, but I could improve it by _____." The purpose of brainstorming is to kick-start your imagination to generate ideas. So browse the Internet, go to the library, visit museums, flip through magazines, look at advertisements, take a walk outside and look, listen, taste, feel, and smell the world around you. Dive into new or exciting topics that can hold your attention and see what you learn.

IT SOUNDS LIKE THE COLLAGES I LIKE TO MAKE.

Exactly. Inspiration can be anywhere and it helps to browse deep and wide to find it. Your brain sees patterns and connects dots in ways that may not seem obvious at first, so it's okay to daydream a little. For the puppies out there, now's a good time to chase a few butterflies and see where they take you. If you're more of a kitten, brainstorming can be a fun, low-stress way to get your paws on that new toy.

MAKE IT PRETTY!

Whiteboards, corkboards, colorful note cards, thumbtacks, Post-its, and stickers. Highlighters, markers, crayons, and colored pencils. Notebooks, binders, legal pads, construction paper. Magazine pages, postcards, photos, design patterns, color swatches, movie posters, cover art. Quotes, song lyrics, sayings, symbols. These are all excellent tools to have on hand for a brainstorming session. Put up an inspiration board, write out your ideas on note cards and pin them up, think of a clever title or name for your product, and write it on your wall (check with an adult before writing *on* the wall, though!). Draw the main character in a new game or an idea for a logo. Write out your leading questions and hang them high on your board. Write down all the answers that come up and highlight them in different colors. Visual aids are great tools for getting your creative thinking flowing.

HAVE A LITTLE HELP

But do you want to know what the most important, extra-special secret weapon of brainstorming is?

YOUR FRIENDS! COLLABORATION, or working together, is key to brainstorming. Tossing around ideas in a group setting lets people build on what's being said. Not only is it fun, but different people bring different viewpoints that can take an idea in a direction you may not have considered. Collaborating helps ideas grow by putting many minds on a problem. And don't forget that part of brainstorming is getting out as many ideas as possible. It's not a time to be self-conscious or worry about whether or not your idea is good. Likewise, you shouldn't feel like you have to stop and evaluate anyone else's suggestions. The point is to get thoughts to flow freely, then make decisions about them later. So treating everyone's ideas with kindness and creating a safe non-judgmental place to express your ideas are a super important part of the process.

DESIGN

Once the brainstorm-y skies have cleared and you start to see a glimmer of an idea about what you want to make, it's time to start prioritizing. This means narrowing down your idea to something you:

A) Want to do

B) Can do

and

C) Think is worth doing

The best way to figure out if your idea checks these boxes is to ask yourself some valuable questions about what you will be making. So let's play the game of . . .

DIALING IN YOUR DESIGN

Making decisions about what and how to design is like choosing your path in a role-playing video game. Think of this as Level 1 in a video game.

> START

LEVEL 1:
DO WE NEED IT?

Think about something you wish you had—a product or service that would be fun or useful. Is it an app to help students keep track of homework deadlines? Is it a game that teaches teens about the dangers of texting while driving? Is it a new filter for photos or videos? Try to iden-

tify a need that is not already being filled and think of how your product can meet that need.

ANSWER: YES.
CONGRATS! A GOOD IDEA!

> CONTINUE

ANSWER: NOT SURE.
KEEP BRAINSTORMING.

> REPLAY

LEVEL 2:
DOES IT EXIST ALREADY?

How do we know if our product already exists? Research! Look for similar projects online, in stores, or anywhere the product might be available. Try to find out if there is anything close to your idea already out there.

ANSWER: NO.
CONGRATS! A NEW
USEFUL PRODUCT!

> CONTINUE

ANSWER: YES.
CAN WE MAKE IT BETTER?
KEEP RESEARCHING.

> REPLAY

If this was your answer, it's a good idea to look more closely at the products that already exist to see if they can be improved. Read reviews, talk to friends and family members about features they'd like to see in products they use. Determine whether the product could be better tailored to a certain user: kids or teens, for example. Remember you can still find a need and fill it, even if there's competition.

LEVEL 3:
WILL THEY WANT IT?

Ask yourself if there is a demand for this idea. Will people want to use it? Do they need it? Will they like it? This question is important for both brand-new products and existing products you are trying to improve. So how do you find out if people will like or need your product? Ask around. Talk with friends, teachers, and family. Be able to explain your idea in a sentence or two or show them a sketch and see what the response is—wild enthusiasm or a shoulder shrug and a "meh"? Write down the feedback you get and let it help steer your design.

ANSWER: YES.
WHO IS IT FOR?
KEEP RESEARCHING.

> CONTINUE

People want your product, great! Now think about who those people are. Who is going to use your program, app, or robot? How will they be using it? If you are tailoring a product to a certain group of people, how will that change the look and style of the product? Will it change how the product works? For example, the instructions for a spelling bee game for kindergartners would be very different from a puzzle game for teens. Think carefully about your user and let that inform your design.

ANSWER: NOT SURE.
LISTEN TO THEIR FEEDBACK
AND TRY ADAPTING.

> REPLAY

LEVEL 4:
DO I WANT TO DO IT?

This is a big one. Ask yourself, "Am I interested enough to stick with this project?" Is it doable? Do you have the time and attention to commit to it? Is it something small you can code in between soccer practice, piano lessons, and homework? Or is it a much larger app that will take up all of your free time? Make sure you have the time to spare. More important, are you excited about the idea? You may discover the need for an app to re-mind you when it's time to trim your toenails, but that doesn't mean you want to spend your nights and weekends working on it. Any project re-quires a time commitment. If you will be spending a lot of time making something, you should believe in what you are doing and have the time and attention it will take to see the project through.

ANSWER: YES.	ANSWER: NOT SURE.
CONGRATS!	KEEP BRAINSTORMING.
› GO TO THE NEXT LEVEL	› GO BACK TO THE START

YOU DID IT!!!

VISUALIZE THE PRIZE

By now, hopefully you have an idea for something. Maybe it's not a new idea, but you have an interesting twist on something that will make it really useful to a certain user. You've asked your questions, done your research, and are ready to start working on the idea.

Now imagine you are given a 1,000-piece jigsaw puzzle, but instead of a picture on the box to show you what you are trying to make, the box is blank. Think about how much harder it would be to put the pieces together in the correct order without a picture to guide you. That's why the next useful step when starting your project is to VISUALIZE the idea by drawing it out in picture form or as a diagram. In other words, it's time to design!

DESIGNERS: *Google the definition of designer and you'll see this: "a person who plans the form, look, or workings of something before it's being made or built, typically by drawing it in detail."*

There are costume designers, graphic designers, and product designers. If you can build it, someone was in charge of designing it. In computer programming, the designer isn't always the coder. There are designers who specialize in USER EXPERIENCE, which means creating products by thinking about how people will use and interact with them. There are also designers who specialize in graphics and in hardware design. While not all designers have to know how to code to work on a program (though it's ideal if they do!), it's very important for coders to understand design.

WIREFRAMES

Wireframing is a technique for drawing what the pages of a website or app will look like. WIREFRAMES can vary in the level of detail, but no matter how simple or complicated, they are the first step in visualizing your end product.

Hand draw your wireframes or make them on the computer. How complicated is up to you!

MENU		
PHOTO + HEADLINE		
PHOTO + LINK 1	PHOTO + LINK 2	PHOTO + LINK 3
PHOTO + LINK 4	PHOTO + LINK 5	PHOTO + LINK 6

STORYBOARDS, SKETCHES, DIAGRAMS, DRAWING

Storyboards are like little comics that show the action of your application. One way that storyboards are often used is in video game design.

They show the action of a game shot by shot and can be a helpful way to draw the different levels and looks of a video game. You can make them simple—to just explain the location and rules of a certain level in a game—or very detailed, to draw the look and action for characters.

Even if you are not making an app or game, it can still help to draw your idea before you get started. Building a robot? Make a drawing of what it might look like. Draw a diagram of the different commands it can understand and the responses it will make. Creating interactive jewelry or a smart watch? Sketch out the shape, size, and color. How big will it be? Will it be adjustable? Annotate the image to point out features and functions for which you'll write code. However you choose to do it, visualizing your idea will give you a great road map for when you begin to build.

FEATURE CREEP

There is one last thing to talk about in this part of the design phase—something that gives even experienced coders nightmares. It's the dreaded Creature Feep!!

Oops, not Creature Feep—FEATURE CREEP. This isn't an oozing swamp monster, but it can be just as scary. Feature creep is when you get so excited about your design, you keep adding more and more features. (Puppies in the Park, I'm talking to you!) While it may be great to add cool extras and services, it can be kind of like putting too many toppings on your ice cream sundae; at a certain point, it just becomes gross. With feature creep, if you add too many bells and whistles you risk making your project hard to use and almost impossible to code. The best strategy is to start simple and focus on only the most important features—the ones you need to make the product work. You can always add features once your project is up and running.

Think of it this way: You're in math class and your teacher asks you to write an equation that equals 4. You could write $1+1+1+2-1=4$ or you could write, $1+3=4$ or $2+2=4$, or $2^2=4$.

There are a lot of different ways to get to the same answer, but some are simpler and more efficient than others.

It's the same with your design. You are aiming for the clearest, most direct path to your end product. With a simple design you can spend more of your attention making it work well and look and feel good, instead of getting lost in the swamp of too many features.

With your design started, it's time to start thinking about how you will actually build your project.

This is the next step of project planning, and it's not about the look of the product, but figuring out how to make it work and what code to write it in.

So let's say good-bye to brainstorming and design and say HELLO, WORLD!

PEANUT BUTTER MUFFINS

CRACKING THE "CODE"

OKAY, YOU KNOW ABOUT BRAINSTORMING AND YOU KNOW ABOUT design. Now we're ready to start building, right?

We're almost there. But before you begin writing code there are a couple more really important steps to take that will help you anticipate problems, fix mistakes, and save you a lot of time and trouble in the long run.

GO WITH THE FLOW

The best way to build anything is to follow a plan. Writers make an outline. Painters start with a sketch. Engineers use blueprints. Dressmakers follow a pattern. It's the same for coding, but in coding the plan is called an APPLICATION FLOW. An application flow is kind of like a visualized algorithm. It's a flow chart that outlines all the steps you will need to get your program to complete its objective. You can write it down on a piece of paper or up on a whiteboard, or you can put it in the notes of your different wireframes. The point is to write it down and look at it closely.

WAIT, WHAT'S AN OBJECTIVE AGAIN?

The objective is what you want the program to do—the task the program is designed to complete. In the same way that brainstorming helps you figure out *what* you are going to build, an application flow helps you map out *how* it's going to work. Especially when the algorithm for your program begins to get complicated.

Let's try one. What's something we want to make?

HOW ABOUT A SOFTBALL VIDEO GAME FOR YOUR PHONE?

Perfect. So imagine we've built our wire-frame and have an idea of what the game will look like. Now let's think about how it will work. What's the first step in the game?

A PLAYER STEPS UP TO BAT!

Then what?

WAIT, THIS IS HARD. THERE ARE A LOT OF DIFFERENT THINGS THAT CAN HAPPEN WHEN YOU GET TO THE PLATE.

That's true. You could hit a single, double, triple, or a home run. You can strike out. The pitcher can throw you a ball, the outfielder can catch your pop fly, or the shortstop can tag you before you get to a base. . . .

You've just made an important observation: if we try to replicate the real game of softball, it would need a very complicated algorithm, something that would take weeks and weeks to code. That might be a bigger job than we're ready for, so before we even start mapping an application flow, perhaps we should simplify things. (See that? We identified and solved a problem before we even started coding. That's why we plan!)

So how about this? Here are some rules for a **SIMPLE SOFTBALL GAME.**

1   The away team will bat first.

2   Each player has three tries to hit the ball. If they hit the ball, they get one point for their team. If they miss, they get a strike. Three strikes and you're out.

3   Three outs, and it's the next team's turn.

4   Each team will go up to bat seven times (so fourteen total turns).

5   At the end of the game, we'll check who won.

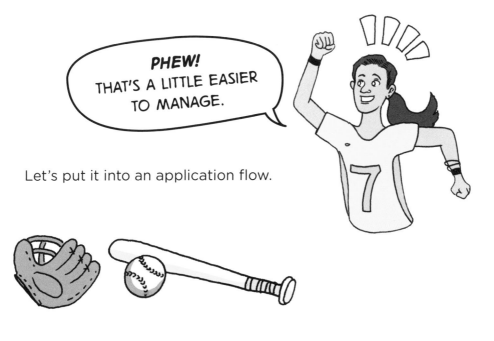

PHEW!
THAT'S A LITTLE EASIER
TO MANAGE.

Let's put it into an application flow.

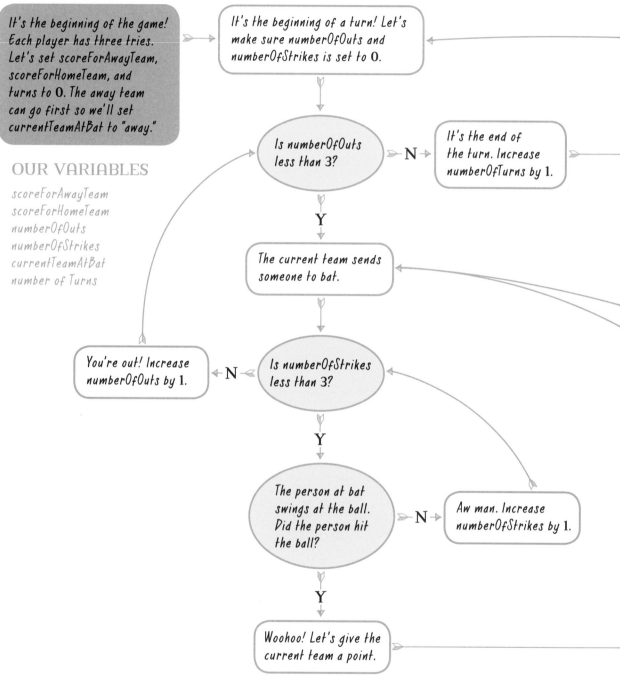

★ START HERE ★

It's the beginning of the game! Each player has three tries. Let's set scoreForAwayTeam, scoreForHomeTeam, and turns to 0. The away team can go first so we'll set currentTeamAtBat to "away."

OUR VARIABLES

scoreForAwayTeam
scoreForHomeTeam
numberOfOuts
numberOfStrikes
currentTeamAtBat
number of Turns

It's the beginning of a turn! Let's make sure numberOfOuts and numberOfStrikes is set to 0.

Is numberOfOuts less than 3?

N

It's the end of the turn. Increase numberOfTurns by 1.

Y

The current team sends someone to bat.

You're out! Increase numberOfOuts by 1.

N

Is numberOfStrikes less than 3?

Y

The person at bat swings at the ball. Did the person hit the ball?

N

Aw man. Increase numberOfStrikes by 1.

Y

Woohoo! Let's give the current team a point.

SOFTBALL
(SIMPLIFIED)

Is numberOfTurns less than 14?

Y → Let's switch currentTeamAtBat to the other team; it's the other team's turn now so let's go back to the beginning of a turn.

N

It's the end of the game! Let's check who won.

Are scoreForAwayTeam and scoreForHomeTeam equal to each other?

N → Is scoreForAwayTeam greater than scoreForHomeTeam?

N → THE HOME TEAM WON!

Y → IT'S A TIE!

Y → THE AWAY TEAM WON!

Increase scoreForAwayTeam by 1.

Y

Is currentTeamAtBat set to "away"?

N → Increase scoreForHomeTeam by 1.

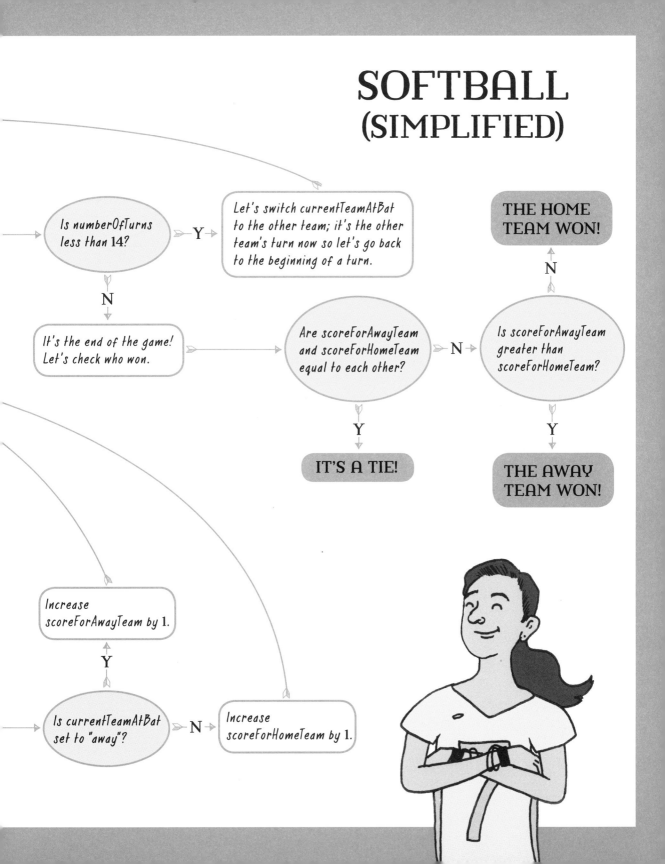

What's the first thing you notice about this?

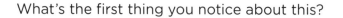

> THERE ARE *A LOT* OF DIFFERENT BRANCHES AND PATHWAYS. *IT'S NOT A STRAIGHT LINE.*

Exactly. Algorithms are rarely nice, straight lines. More often than not, an application flow looks kind of like a subway or train map. It starts with a main line, but then all these branches appear that take you in different directions, depending on what the user does (hits a ball, strikes out, etc.). It's kind of like those books where you can choose what happens next while you read—each choice takes you to a different ending to the story. This means that, as a programmer, you're not just writing one set of instructions with a beginning, middle, and end. Your algorithm has to include instructions for all the different possible outcomes in your program. This is exactly why creating an application flow is so helpful. It lets you see the pathways a program can take and gives you an idea of the different pieces of code you will need to write.

> I REQUEST ACCESS TO PARTICIPATE IN THE MULTIPLAYER ACTIVITY THAT UTILIZES NON-FIRM SPHERES.

> UMM . . . YOU MEAN YOU WANT TO PLAY SOFTBALL?

> AFFIRMATIVE.

LABELING YOUR FLOW

Once you've sketched out an idea of the flow of game and the directions the different pathways will take, it's time to identify which paths are loops and which are conditionals, and, of course, what your variables are.

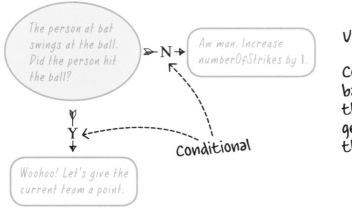

Variable: numberOfStrikes

Conditional: If the batter hits the ball, then the batter's team gets a point. Otherwise, the team gets a strike.

Variable:
numberOfStrikes

Loop: Person at bat continues to swing at the ball until numberOfStrikes is 3, or until the person gets a hit.

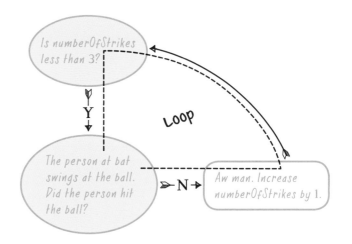

WRITE IT OUT

You've just gotten through what may be the hardest part of the design! You've planned out your program and labeled it; now it's time to start writing it out. This is still not the actual coding part, but it's what we like to call pseudocode. You've already seen plenty of pseudocode in this book so far (the Lunch Line Algorithm in Chapter 3, for example.) All pseudocode does is use normal, everyday writing to spell out exactly what you will be coding as very precise instructions.

Basically, it's like writing out your algorithm in robot talk. You can see that the conditionals, loops, and variables are all clearly written out in this code.

> BUT WHY SPEND ALL THAT TIME WRITING OUT PSEUDOCODE? WE ALREADY HAVE AN APPLICATION FLOW TO TELL US WHAT HAPPENS NEXT— WHY NOT JUST WRITE THE ACTUAL CODE?

Pseudocode lets you write out the LOGIC of the program—the steps you need to take to get from the beginning to the end of your program—without getting lost in the SYNTAX of the code. The syntax is kind of like the spelling, spacing, and formatting part of writing the code.

If you write your detailed application flow as pseudocode, when it's time to actually code, you don't have to think about what happens next or whether or not it's going to work, and you won't get distracted by rules

of the programming language. You just have one job: to translate your pseudocode into actual code.

At the start of the game, both teams' scores are set to 0 and the away team goes first.

```
scoreForHomeTeam = 0
scoreForAwayTeam = 0

turnNumber = 0
```
It's the beginning of the 0th turn.

```
teamAtBat = "away"
while (turns < 14):
    outs = 0
```
While turns is less than 14 (7 for each team), teams will take turns.

```
    while (outs < 3):
```
Until number of outs is 3.

The current team will send a player to bat and they have 0 strikes.

```
        strikes = 0
        player.next()
```
Until that player has 3 strikes they will keep swinging at the ball.

```
        while (strikes < 3):
            hit = player.bats()
            if (hit == True):
```

If they hit the ball, their team gets a point.

```
                if (currentTeamAtBat == "away"):
                    scoreForAwayTeam = scoreForAwayTeam + 1
                else:
                    scoreForHomeTeam = scoreForHomeTeam + 1
            else:
                strikes = strikes + 1
```

If they miss the ball, they get a strike.

WHEN I DECORATE A CAKE I DRAW MY DESIGN, THEN FROST THE CAKE AND TRACE THE ART ONTO IT. I LAY OUT EVERYTHING FIRST SO WHEN I START ACTUALLY DECORATING, I'M NOT THINKING ABOUT THE DESIGN, JUST BUILDING IT.

THE SECRET INGREDIENT—PROBLEM-SOLVING

Making a cake is like coding, and so is following a dress pattern, or coloring in a sketch you've already drawn, or assembling a toy. These are all step-by-step processes that follow a plan.

Remember, coding is really just problem-solving—taking a big task and figuring out how to break it into smaller, doable pieces using computational thinking. Once you've done that, your next step is to choose a programming language to write your code in, and you're ready to go.

So let's choose a programming language.

UMM . . . I'M NOT SURE I UNDERSTAND WHAT A PROGRAMMING LANGUAGE IS AND WHY THERE ARE DIFFERENT ONES.

At a mechanical level, most computers operate in a very simple language called BINARY. Binary code turns numbers, words, and even images and sounds into a series of 1's and 0's that can be sent through the computer as electrical pulses. Each digit of these BINARY NUMBERS is called a BIT.

> BUT WHY DO COMPUTERS USE **BINARY** NUMBERS AND NOT NORMAL NUMBERS AND WORDS LIKE WE ALREADY USE?

Computers are made up of millions and millions of electrical circuits. These circuits, just like a light switch, have two modes. They are either turned *on* or turned *off*. By using just two numbers—1 to equal *on* and 0 to equal *off*—computers can simplify trillions of different combinations of numbers and commands into a series of just two electrical pulses.

Think about what a code, any code, actually is. In general terms, a code is a way of using words, numbers, letters, or symbols to represent something else.

Sometimes people uses codes to keep a secret and hide the real meaning of their words, like coded messages used by spies and the military. Other times people use codes to take complicated phrases or information and

HELLO WORLD

Morse Code

simplify them to communicate faster. Nautical flags are a great example. This code uses color and patterns as a quick way to visually communicate complicated instructions over long distances at sea.

Binary code has a similar function. It simplifies a complex communication system into just two symbols. There are actually lots of different kinds of binary codes that humans use outside of computing. Morse Code, which was used on the first telegraphs lines and by ships, uses just two symbols: dots and dashes representing short or long sounds or light flashes to spell out words. Braille, the alphabet visually impaired people read with their hands, uses a series of raised and un-raised dots to represent letters. It is also a form of binary.

Braille

SO THE MOST COMPLICATED, ELABORATE COMPUTER PROCESSES IN THE WORLD ARE JUST TURNING MILLIONS AND MILLIONS OF LITTLE ELECTRICAL SWITCHES ON OR OFF?

Yep, basically. Pretty amazing, right?

DO YOU SPEAK BINARY?

Imagine if you had to write out all those commands as 1's and 0's. It would be almost impossible to keep track of because binary code is not intuitive to people used to reading and writing in human languages. This is why programming languages are so important.

And that's why a breakthrough in 1952 changed the history of computing. That was when a computer scientist invented the first operational COMPILER, a special program that could translate alphanumeric input (a-b-c's and 1-2-3's) that humans could read and understand into the binary language of computers. This revolutionized the world of computer science, allowing engineers to develop programming languages or "code" that was much easier for humans to write and work with. So who was this incredible computer scientist?

Computer Pioneer
GRACE MURRAY HOPPER

Modern coding wouldn't exist if it weren't for the mind of Grace Hopper, often called "Amazing Grace." In 1941 Grace was a married mathematics professor at Vassar College. Then, on December 7, the Japanese bombed Pearl Harbor, sending the United States into World War II. This major world event would also be a turning point in Grace's life. Shortly after the war broke out, she divorced her husband and joined the U.S. Navy, where she threw her impressive mathematical mind into the war effort. This is where she began her career as a computer scientist, which she continued long after the war ended. Grace would go on to work in the private sector, inventing compilers and working with other computer scientists to develop programming languages, most notably COBOL. Without her work, modern programing and the software development that allows everyday people to operate computers would not have been possible.

Thanks to Grace Hopper, we can now use compilers to take programming languages that humans can read and understand and convert them into binary, a language that computers understand.

CHOOSING A PROGRAMMING LANGUAGE

Programming languages are similar to human languages: there are tons of them and each one has its own unique way to write the same thing. To get an idea of how many programming languages are out there, google "hello world code."

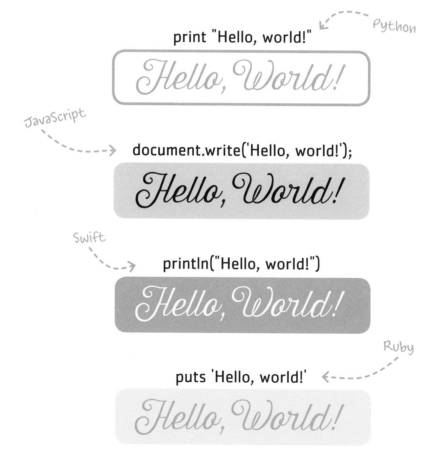

C#

```csharp
using System;
class Program
{
    public static void Main(string[] args)
    {
        Console.WriteLine("Hello, world!");
    }
}
```

Hello, World!

Java

```java
public class HelloWorld {
    public static void main(String[] args) {
        System.out.println("Hello, World");
    }
}
```

Hello, World!

As you can see, there are lots of different ways to write the same thing.

This simple program, asking your computer to write "hello world," is what people use to check that a programming language is working correctly, but it also illustrates just how many different programming languages are out there.

WOW, WITH SO MANY LANGUAGES OUT THERE, HOW DO WE DECIDE WHICH ONE TO LEARN?

That depends on what you want to do. Certain languages are better for certain tasks. While there's no hard and fast rule about what to use for any given project, here's a helpful guide.

Coding Language	Uses
SCRATCH Visual coding system. Uses colored blocks of code and premade graphics to create easy games and apps. Great place for beginners to start.	Video games, art, animation
LEGO MINDSTORMS NXT This language is used by the FIRST Robotics League, a massive organization that gets students involved in robotics.	Robotics
PYTHON General-purpose language that can be used for quite a bit including scientific applications.	Web and apps, software development, games, robotics
HTML/CSS These are not programming languages. They are markup languages. A markup language is a way to design and present text, like the headers and writing on a website. It's also what you use to add structure/content (HTML) and style (CSS) to websites. They're not programming languages because they don't remember/repeat/decide, but are used to lay out and arrange content on a page.	Web and apps
JAVASCRIPT Not the same as Java, despite the similar name. This is the programming language used to make the web interactive. There are a lot of libraries built on top of JavaScript, the biggest one being jQuery, that are typically free to use and contribute to.	Web and apps

Coding Language	Uses
ARDUINO PROGRAMMING LANGUAGE This is the language for programming Arduino microcontrollers, built on C++ (a general purpose programming language).	Robotics
JAVA What the current high school advanced placement computer science curriculum uses. Another general purpose language, what you'd use to make an Android app.	Web and apps, games
SWIFT Used for making iOS apps. Also need XCode, which is a program for Mac. Very new, young, and exciting language, has only been around since 2014.	Apps
PROCESSING This is described as a flexible software sketchbook and a great language for art and design.	Video games, art, animation
C A historic and widely known language. It's a good language for when speed matters. It is a "systems language," meaning there are few barriers between you and the 1's and 0's of the system.	Libraries, software
C# (pronounced C-sharp) Different from C, but was originally meant to be C-like. Useful for game development.	Video games
MAYA EMBEDDED LANGUAGE This is a language used in the software Maya, which is similar to what they use at Pixar to do 3-D animation. Within Maya, you can write Python scripts to generate 3-D models as well as animations.	Animation, art, video games

To get started programming with these languages and more, visit GirlsWhoCode.com/books!

BUILDING

Once you've narrowed down the language you want to work in, it's time to start building. In other words, it's finally time to start writing your code.

YESSS! FINALLY!

QUICK TIP: *Keep It Tidy and Back It Up!*

As you start to build, you will be making new files and keeping track of old files. One of the best gifts you can give yourself is keeping your files organized and tidy. Come up with a naming system that includes a date or version number and stick to it. Name things the same way every time. Back up your work daily to an external drive or online account so you have a backup separate from your computer. Having good work habits helps you find material and fix issues as soon as they come up.

So here we are—you're coding! If you've walked through all your design and planning steps beforehand, building should just be a matter of writing out your algorithms in code. Easy-peasy, right?

What could possibly go wrong?

DEBUGGING

LET'S IMAGINE THAT YOU'VE WORKED YOUR WAY THROUGH A COUple of online tutorials and have learned a coding language. There you are at your laptop, coding your little heart out, writing strings and lines and variables and loops, adding parameters and functions. You are building like crazy. It's going great—you're a coding all-star! You finish your last line and run your program—

And, like a pimple on school picture day, up it pops:

> **THE DREADED ERROR MESSAGE.**

Time to get to the real work of coding: testing and . . .

DEBUGGING

It's one thing to write code; it's another to get it to run. And when it's time to test your program, you're almost guaranteed to hit some kind of snag the first time you run it. In computer science, when something isn't working in a program it's called a bug. Finding, identifying, and fixing the problem is called DEBUGGING.

Remember our friend the inventor of the compiler, Grace Murray Hopper? She coined the term "debugging" when, according to the story, she traced the cause of a malfunction in her computer to an actual moth that had gotten into the hardware. To fix the problem, she had to "debug" her computer, literally. That's how the word was born.

SYNTAX OR LOGIC

Assuming there isn't an insect flying around inside your laptop, most code problems can be traced to one of two types of errors.

A SYNTAX ERROR is a problem with how you wrote your code. You left out a letter, symbol, space, or punctuation mark.

A LOGIC ERROR is a problem with the flow of your application. You are asking the computer to do something that doesn't make sense or that it simply can't do.

Here are some examples written in Javascript.

INCORRECT CODE	CORRECT CODE
`var myName = Leila";`	`var myName = "Leila";`

SYNTAX ERROR

This is a syntax error because in Javascript (and most languages) strings like Leila's name need to be surrounded by quotes on both sides. Syntax errors are very common in coding and can be caused by missing semicolons, incorrect spacing, or typos.

INCORRECT CODE	CORRECT CODE
`var numberOfPeople = 0;`	`var numberOfPeople = 4;`
`var pizzaSlices = 12;`	`var pizzaSlices = 12;`
`pizzaSlicesPerPerson = pizzaSlices / numberOfPeople;`	`pizzaSlicesPerPerson = pizzaSlices / numberOfPeople;`

DIVIDE BY ZERO ERROR

We have a variable for the number of people at a party and the number of pizza slices. We then try and divide pizza slices by number of people to find out how many slices to give to each person. However, just like us, computers don't know how to divide by zero so invite some people to your party!

INCORRECT CODE	CORRECT CODE
`if (myAge = 12) {`	`if (myAge == 12) {`
`    alert("Only one more year until I'm a teen!");`	`    alert("Only one more year until I'm a teen");`
`}`	`}`

USE DOUBLE EQUAL SIGNS WITH "IF" STATEMENTS

When you have a condition in an "if" statement, you use double equal signs to check if things are equal to one another because a single equal sign is used for setting variables. In the example on the left, rather than checking if myAge is equal to 12, we are setting myAge to 12!

INCORRECT CODE	CORRECT CODE
`pizzaSlicesEaten = 0;`	`pizzaSlicesEaten = 0;`
`do {`	`do {`
`    self.eat("pizzaSlice");`	`    self.eat("pizzaSlice");`
	`    pizzaSlicesEaten = pizzaSlicesEaten + 1;`
`} while (pizzaSlicesEaten < 3);`	`} while (pizzaSlicesEaten < 3);`

INFINITE LOOP

We have a loop that tells us to keep eating pizza slices as long as pizzaSlicesEaten is less than 3. However, in the code on the left we'll be caught in an infinite loop because we forgot to increase the number of pizzaSlicesEaten each time through the loop. We'd be eating pizza forever!

SO HOW DO YOU FIX THEM?

There are a few helpful strategies you can apply. But first you need to *find* the error. Any time you want to check if there is an error in your code, start by running your program. If there is a problem, usually whatever coding language you are working in will give you an error message that indicates where and why the error is happening.

The next step is to *identify* what kind of error you've made: syntax or logic. If your code runs but doesn't do what you want, that's a logic error. If your code doesn't run because you made a typo, that's a syntax error. If you have an error message, that can provide a big clue, but you have to understand what the message means.

HOW DO YOU FIGURE THAT OUT?

Don't forget, you can always ask for help. I recommend following this little "Asking for Help" guide.

FIRST: YOUR BEAUTIFUL BRAIN

That's right. Start by asking yourself. See if you can figure it out on your own. Some error messages are self-explanatory, or you might be able to find the error right away by simply going back to the line the message lists.

THEN: THE INTERNET

Ahhh . . . the Internet, that wonderful world of search engines and message boards and tech blogs and how-to videos; there's bound to be a solution there. Try Googling your error message to see if you can get an answer to help you solve it. You can also look up your error message in the programming language's **DOCUMENTATION**—this is basically the instruction manual, technical details, and user guide for a programming language. You can usually find a link to this information on the programming language's home page.

NEXT: YOUR FRIENDS

Still having trouble? Ask a friend, preferably one you've been collaborating with or who is working on a similar project. Chances are, your friend has already come across the same issue that you have and has worked through a solution. I'm sure she or he will be happy to share that solution—that's what friends are for!

LAST: YOUR TEACHER OR MENTOR

Last but not least, you can always ask a teacher or mentor. Your mentor can be an older sibling, friend, or neighbor who knows how to code, or you can connect with one through the Girls Who Code community. Not only are teachers—especially the ones teaching you coding—fantastic sources of all kinds of information, but they also tend to love helping students overcome hurdles and keep learning (go figure).

BUT WHY DO WE HAVE TO DO IT IN THAT ORDER? WHY NOT JUST ASK YOUR TEACHER FIRST, IF THAT PERSON MIGHT HAVE THE ANSWER?

Think about it this way. Fast-forward twenty years. You're working in your dream job (maybe even in tech). You've been given a great new assignment: helping your boss with a big project. You come across a few things you don't understand in a report. Are you going to e-mail your boss every time you have a

question? Or will your try to solve the problem on your own first by re-searching it and checking in with teammates?

> I GUESS I'D WANT TO TRY TO DO IT MYSELF SO MY BOSS KNOWS I CAN AND BECAUSE IT'S PART OF MY RESPONSIBILITY.

If you don't understand something, it's always better to ask for help than to pretend you've got it covered. But it's important to develop self-reliance. By learning to solve problems on your own, you get better at what you are doing, you take responsibility for your work, and you build confidence every time you solve a tricky dilemma on your own.

Which brings us to our next debugging strategy.

RUBBER DUCK IT

Got a tough problem? Try the rubber duck method: talk through the problem out loud to whoever's willing to listen—your friend, your mom, your friend's mom, the mail carrier, or, if all else fails, a rubber ducky sitting on your desk. Your listener may not have any useful advice

> HMM . . . I SEE WHAT YOU'RE GOING FOR. HAVE YOU TRIED . . .

for you—their response isn't the point. By explaining the problem out loud, you can sometimes see answers you were missing before. In the same way that painters often step back from their work to look at the whole picture before they make another stroke, talking out your issue lets you step away from the details to see the bigger picture and, hopefully, a possible solution.

ERROR DETECTIVE

This strategy requires your pointer finger, a pen, some paper, and good old-fashioned detective work. Start at the beginning of your code and trace it with your finger, line by line. Look for syntax errors as you go. Make a list of the variables' names you come across on your paper and track how they change on each line of the program. Make sure they're correct and consistent. Track them on your paper and compare them to your wireframes and application flow. See if there is an error in your logic or something you missed.

PRINT FUNCTION

Programming languages often have a built-in function called something like print. For any language, you can always check the documentation or do a quick search to find out what print (or any given function) is called. You can use this function to display the values of different variables at different times throughout your code. Run one every five or ten lines to see if that bundle of code is working correctly. It might help to print out

a message to let you know what "if" statements are being displayed as true. This method basically lets you track where in the code the problem is happening. It's a way to isolate the problem by testing batches of code.

INTEGRATED DEVELOPMENT ENVIRONMENT (IDE)

An IDE is a piece of software to help you write code. It basically has a TEXT EDITOR, the window where you write your code, a compiler, and its own system for debugging code all in one. This can be helpful in a lot of ways. Many IDEs will catch syntax errors automatically and highlight them as you write. Then you'll know right away if you made a simple typo or spelling mistake without having to search through your code. They also often have autocomplete and automated functions to help you code faster and reduce accidental typos and mistakes.

TAKE A BREAK

Sometimes when you really get stuck, taking a walk, getting a snack, or simply sleeping on it can be a huge help. Just because we aren't actively working on something doesn't mean our brains aren't still rearranging puzzle pieces and working on a solution. In fact, getting lots of rest; eating healthy, nourishing foods; spending time with friends and family; and getting fresh air and exercise are all key elements to solving any problem

because they are essential ingredients to clear thinking. And clear thinking helps you see and avoid problems in the first place.

Last but not least, one of the most important strategies for solving any problem . . .

EMBRACE IMPERFECTION

As women, we are constantly hearing all kinds of conflicting messages about what we can and cannot do. We're supposed to be good girls, be nice, follow rules, be friendly, be kind, be helpful, be, well . . . PERFECT! Well, take it from me, as a grown-up, a professional woman, and a mother: NOBODY IS PERFECT. I'm going to say it again just in case it didn't sink in—wait, let me get some help . . .

AFFIRMATIVE.
NOBODY IS PERFECT.
NOT EVEN ROBOTS.

What does this have to do with coding? Everything. You're probably used to being praised for getting your work right and doing well and being "good." So what happens when you get something wrong? Or you make a mistake, just like everyone in the world does when they are learning something new (and even when they are not)?

Women (and men, too) can often be really mean to themselves. We get mad at ourselves and frustrated; we even call ourselves names or think stuff like, *That was so dumb, I can't believe I can't get this, what's wrong with me?* You would never talk to your best friend that way, or a teacher or parent, so why do it to yourself? If you want to be successful in any pursuit—playing a sport, mastering an instrument, learning a language, taking a test, building a robot—don't try to be *perfect*. Instead, be *brave*.

Take a chance! Every time you get something wrong, you learn how to do it right.

But most of all, be *kind* to yourself. Forgive yourself for mistakes, tell yourself you *can* do it and you *will* figure it out and it's *okay* not to be perfect. Then get back to the things that will actually make you better: *practice*, *patience*, and *perseverance*.

You can do it. Deep down, I bet there's a part of you that already knows you've got this. Let *that* voice do the talking.

And remember: Being in the moment, learning, getting your hands dirty—that's what being a girl who codes is all about.

The reward of doing something new is not just the end product—it's the feeling you get in the middle of it, when you're using your beautiful brain, your bravery, and your gift of clear thinking to figure it out.

So are you ready to start building your own amazing inventions with code? Let's start with a popular favorite. You play them online, on your phone, on your gaming system . . . and guess what? Now you can make them yourself!

7

VIDEO GAMES

HOPEFULLY BY NOW YOUR BRAINS ARE BRIMMING WITH IDEAS FOR projects. So let's talk about some of our options. What should we make?

I WANT TO KNOW MORE ABOUT MAKING *VIDEO GAMES!*

Whether they have you catching creatures, crushing candy, racing carts, building worlds out of blocks, solving puzzles, finding treasure, or earning points to reach new levels, video games are one of the most popular things you can do with code. They're also a great way to tell stories and educate players. Video games are a perfect project to get you started with code because you can begin with a simple concept and add details to your game as your coding skills get stronger.

HOW DO WE FIGURE OUT WHAT KIND OF GAME TO MAKE? **THERE ARE SO MANY DIFFERENT KINDS!**

That's true! Game GENRES are groups of games organized by how you play them. Here are just a few . . .

ADVENTURE and ROLE-PLAYING

PUZZLES

ACTION

Simulation

DRIVING/RACING

STRATEGY

Not only are there different genres of games, but you can also create games to serve different purposes. Some are just for fun. Some are designed to teach you something or practice a skill, like a kids' ABC game, math games, puzzles, or problem-solving games. Other games help raise awareness for a cause or are tied to a movie, character, or brand.

Video games can draw on all kinds of interests you might have outside of COMPUTER PROGRAMMING. Are you a good writer? Adventure and role-playing games need well-thought-out stories with characters, scripts, and dialogue. Love sudoku, crosswords, or numbers and shapes? Puzzle games are the perfect way to combine design, problem-solving, and coding. Are you interested in maps, landscapes, and different environments? Simulation games involve all of those things.

> I NEVER REALIZED THERE WERE SO MANY THINGS TO DO WITH VIDEO GAMES. **THIS MAKES IT EVEN HARDER TO KNOW WHERE TO START!**

Let's talk to some of our Girls Who Code about a game they created to see if we can pick up some pointers on VIDEO GAME DEVELOPMENT.

Glory K., Zahraa L., Maria M., and Nany N. from a New York City GWC program created this game as their final project. It's a dress-up game geared

toward girls ages five to twelve, focused on expressing the beauty within *all* skin colors, hair styles, and body types. The game lets you chose a hairstyle, body type, skin color, and profession. Then it gives you interesting facts about women in your chosen field.

Tell us about how you came up with the idea for this game.

GLORY: We got teamed up in the program and I wanted to do something about girl empowerment. Maria, Zahraa, and Nany did as well. I think it was Maria who thought of the dress-up game.

Why a dress-up game?

MARIA: When I was younger, I loved doing all the dress-up games online, but of course they don't look like real people. So that was the basis of our idea: to show all different races and all different styles.

ZAHRAA: I'm black, and growing up, I felt that a lot of those dress-up games, even when they did have a black girl, showed just one brown skin tone—there wasn't a dark-skinned girl, a light-skinned girl, different shades. And the hair was usually really straight and didn't look like mine. I have curly hair and I didn't grow up seeing that, so I didn't think

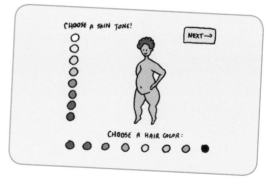

it was beautiful. That's why I wanted to incorporate natural hair, to show girls that you don't have to have straight hair to be beautiful.

Tell us why you included career options as part of the game.

MARIA: We wanted to make it not only about how you look, but also about what you can be and what you can aspire to be.
GLORY: We wanted to make it different from any other dress-up game. There are other games, like pop star dress-up games, or princess dress-up games, but we wanted there to be a bunch of different choices and show that whatever you choose can be good, and whatever field you go into, you can prosper and do well.

Tell us about how you built it. What language did you use and how did you get started?

ZAHRAA: First we used pseudocode and we wrote it out on the board. We didn't actually code—we just talked about it and tried to figure out what program we were going to use.
MARIA: We used JavaScript and also a bit of HTML because this was going to be a website.
GLORY: Nany is also an illustrator, and she made all the drawings.

So this wasn't only computer coding—there was an artistic element, too. What was it like collaborating like that?

MARIA: Since Nany did all the drawing, we all told her our ideas. She incorporated them and then put her own drawing style on it, and it worked out really well.

GLORY: And we all did the code together, so it was definitely very collaborative. We would all be listening to music when we were coding and talking.

ZAHRAA: It was a lot of fun.

MARIA: I think we wrote pretty much every line of code together. We would be on our computers next to each other and I'd be like, "What if we tried this here?" or whatever the code was, and Glory would be like, "That's a good idea. Let's try this here."

What was the hardest part about this project?

MARIA: It was really hard to get the hair colors and skin tones to change. So Nany colored each one individually, and we made space to put each hair and skin color drawing into the code. That way, we didn't have to change them with the code—they were already there.

What was the most satisfying part of this project?

GLORY: We're so passionate about girls and empowering them and making them feel good about themselves, and we were so excited about starting it. Especially because the three of us are best friends and we had such a good time.

MARIA: It feels so awesome to make something from scratch that works, and bring something to life. Before Girls Who Code, I didn't know any computer science, and being able to go from knowing nothing to seeing my idea come together so well and so successfully, and turn into something I was really, really proud of . . . that was incredible.

ZAHRAA: I never coded before this, and to see it work—that was amazing! When we played the game and it worked, I'm pretty sure I actually cried. I learned how to code and I found my best friends.

So what do you think? Any ideas brewing?

I LIKE HOW THEY TURNED THEIR GAME INTO A WAY TO REMIND GIRLS THAT THERE ARE ALL KINDS OF WAYS TO BE BEAUTIFUL AND ALL KINDS OF JOBS YOU CAN BE GOOD AT.

ME TOO, AND IT GIVES ME AN IDEA. I LOVE ANIMALS AND I FOLLOW A LOT OF DIFFERENT CONSERVATION GROUPS THAT WORK TO PROTECT ENDANGERED SPECIES. A GAME COULD BE A GOOD WAY TO GET OTHER KIDS INTERESTED.

YEAH, YOU COULD MAKE A GAME WHERE YOU HAVE TO HELP PROTECT THE HABITAT OF DIFFERENT KINDS OF WILDLIFE, AND THAT WAY PLAYERS CAN LEARN ABOUT WHY THEY'RE ENDANGERED AND WHAT THEY COULD DO TO HELP.

Let's use everything we've learned about getting started and come up with a plan.

What do we need to do first?

You girls are off to a fantastic start. The next step would be figuring out how you earn points to win and lose in the game. What are your loops, variables, and conditionals?

WE COULD USE A VARIABLE TO STORE THE NUMBER OF ANIMALS THAT THE PLAYER HAS SAVED!

```
var totalAnimalsSaved = 15;
```

WHEN THE GAME IS OVER, WE COULD USE AN IF STATEMENT TO CHECK WHETHER OR NOT THE PLAYER HAS SAVED ALL THE ANIMALS.

```
if (totalAnimalsSaved == 15) {
    alert("You saved the animals!");
}
```

As you can tell, there are a lot of steps to creating a video game, but even the simplest games can affect the world in ways you never expect, if you keep yourself open to opportunities. Take it from video game designer Chelsea Howe.

Chelsea Howe

I got into games because I played them my entire life and I loved the idea of creating worlds and stories and characters that other people could experience. So when I learned you could actually make money making video games, I realized that that was definitely the thing I wanted to do with my life.

But making a career designing games wasn't a straightforward path. Chelsea had to create her own opportunities to pursue her passion.

I went to college for languages because a lot of the writers I admired had gone to college to study language and linguistics. When I got there, there was a games program, but it was just two classes. So I wound up applying to a different program so I could design my own major around creating video games.

I had an incredible professor and he saw that I was into this overlap of technology and art and helped me take that leap.

Once in the working world, Chelsea got the opportunity to make the kind of games she'd always wished she had when she was a kid.

I made a bunch of games through college. One of the games I got a publishing contract for, so I got to start my own company with a friend right out of college. At the same time, I was working as a producer making games for the Nintendo Wii back when that was a new, hip thing. I worked on Farmville, a farming simulation game for social networks, back when Farmville had 32 million people playing the game every day. That was this mind-blowing feeling to be able to affect so many people on a game that's about farming and nurturing creatures and plants. I had grown up with a lot of very violent games, so it was really cool to be contributing to something where we had grandmas playing with their grandkids and all sorts of people of all ages playing all over the world.

And it turns out there's a lot more to video games than just having fun. They can actually change lives.

I worked on a game called SuperBetter, which was all about using psychology and elements of games to help people conquer things that were overwhelming in their real lives. One cool thing we found out studying the psychology of games is that when people play games, they know they might win. That's what gets them to try again and again and again. And when you play a game, you have this mind-set: I can get better at this, I can practice, I know I can win. It makes us try really, really hard. We used that to make ways to look at your real life and adopt that mind-set of "If I keep trying, I can overcome this."

So, what's next on the project list?

I'll give you a hint. Coding isn't just fun and games; it can also become a work of art, a comic book with characters that come alive, and technology that can turn a smile into a song.

DIGITAL ART AND DESIGN

IF YOU HAVE INTERESTS AND HOBBIES OUTSIDE OF COMPUTER SCIence, coding can be a great way to build on the activities you are already doing. Girls, how do you want to use coding to do the stuff you're passionate about?

I'D LIKE TO KNOW HOW I CAN USE CODING FOR MY ART PROJECTS. I ALREADY PLAY AROUND WITH PHOTOSHOP AND ILLUSTRATOR, BUT CAN YOU CODE ART?

Absolutely! There are amazing things happening in the world of visual art, design, fashion, music, performance, photography, video, and animation, all using code. After all, just about every art form involves working with some material—whether it's paint or clay, instruments or sound, movement or words—to make something completely new. Coding is just another material you can use. It's a tool for creation, and the sky's the limit for how you want to apply it.

But don't just take it from me. I'll let Tran P. explain how she and her teammates Sandra V., Angela K., and Lily Y. from one of the Girls Who Code programs in San Francisco turned a set of LED lights into an interactive display that flashes in time to music. Perfect for parties and dances, LED It Glow turns music into light. Or, in Tran's words, "If music is what feelings sound like . . . this LED cube is what music looks like."

LED It Glow

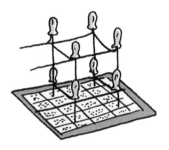

Tell us about your inspiration for LED It Glow.

TRAN: Our group got put together kind of randomly. When we started talking, we realized we all enjoyed music, visual art, and design.

We were talking about how at school dances the lights are old-fashioned disco balls and strobe lights, and wouldn't it be cool to make something better? So we came up with the idea of making our own cube light from scratch that would light up to the beat of the music.

Wow, that's a really unique coding project. How did you get started?

We googled other LED projects and found some really helpful instructions, but they were mostly for 8 x 8 x 8-inch LED cubes. We only had a week for the project, so we decided to do a 4 x 4 x 4 one. We used an Arduino board and coded in Processing.

Where did you get all the materials you needed, the lights and hardware?

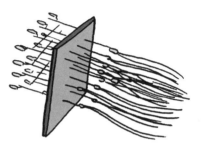

GWC had the Arduino and the LED lights so we just had to gather it together. We got a soldering iron and the wires to connect it. And we had to bend each wire and solder them together side by side, then test that each light worked and test each row.

What was it like to code this project?

I did most of the work with the hardware, and my teammates did the coding. They started by looking up the beats per minute (bpm) to different songs. Then we programmed in patterns based on those bpm. We created a music file to detect the bpm in a song, and we also got it to where it could detect the percussion lines. Once the program detects any of those beats, it lights up patterns that match.

What was the most interesting part of this project?

Connecting the lights to the Arduino and the soldering. Sometimes an LED would break and you'd have to really delicately reach in to change the lightbulb. But it was really satisfying to hardwire the board and work with the soldering iron. It was a new experience and it's such a feeling of accomplishment when you learn something on your own.

Your project really shows how coding can really be a form of artistic expression.

I draw a lot, so it was fun to do a project that was so visual. I'm also really interested in virtual reality and the potential for that in the visual arts. I would tell anybody with an interest in art or a design background to try coding. Have an open mind, because you can do so much, and you can figure out how to make it relate to what you love to do.

~~~~~~~~~~~~~~~~~~~~~~~~~~~~~~~~
~~~~~~~~~~~~~~~~~~~~~~~~~~~~~~~~

LED It Glow is just one idea in a huge range of possibilities when it comes to coding for art, design, and music. Before we start brainstorming, let's look at some other ways artists are working with code.

VISUAL ART

From innovations in animation, film, and photography to 3-D virtual reality landscapes to interactive performance pieces that are coded to change at a touch, art and code are becoming more and more entwined. The emerging field of GENERATIVE ART is at the cutting edge of this work. In this type of art, a computer, in the form of algorithms, generates the imagery. The artists aren't making exact decisions about a picture's shape, style, or color; instead they create an algorithm that lets the computer create within the guidelines the artists set.

Code can also take static artwork and bring it to life. Artists are creating comic books and paintings that animate when you scan over them with your phone's camera. Motion-capture techniques, high-end scanning, and 3-D modeling help artists create amazingly detailed and seamless animated worlds for feature films and shorts.

Data visualization is also a popular branch of coding. Artists use color and shapes to illustrate patterns in data to help us better understand what the information is telling us.

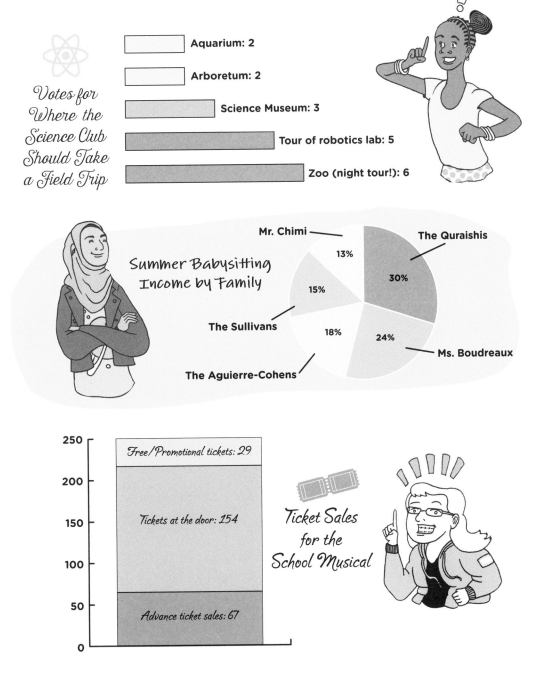

Votes for Where the Science Club Should Take a Field Trip

Aquarium: 2

Arboretum: 2

Science Museum: 3

Tour of robotics lab: 5

Zoo (night tour!): 6

Summer Babysitting Income by Family

Mr. Chimi — 13%

The Quraishis 30%

The Sullivans 15%

Ms. Boudreaux 24%

The Aguierre-Cohens 18%

Ticket Sales for the School Musical

Free/Promotional tickets: 29

Tickets at the door: 154

Advance ticket sales: 67

DESIGN/FASHION

Smart clothing and accessories are huge areas of fashion that combine function and style. Glasses, jewelry, and clothes are being built with processors that can send out your location data to keep you safe. There are athletic clothes that track your heart rate and steps to keep you healthy. You can get many of the functions of your phone in a stylish watch or pair of glasses. There are even LED light-up dresses that let you shine at any party! And all of these designs depend on code.

The invention of 3-D printing has also opened doors in the world of design. In 3-D printing, pliable material is spooled through the printer to lay down multiple super thin layers of material, slice by slice. These layers build up to create a shape, which hardens into a final form. The material is usually plastic, but engineers at Hershey's  have made some fantastic sculptures out of chocolate! Three-dimensional printing allows designers to create elaborate lightweight objects that transform abstract code into solid shapes.

MUSIC

Writing music and writing code aren't all that different; they're both algorithms. Musical notation is a way to encode sound. Not surprisingly,

then, there's a branch of music dedicated to exploring ALGORITHMIC COMPOSITION. This is similar to generative art in that it lets the computer make the music using an algorithm, without the input of a human composer. Coders are using things like the words in books, facial features, and points on a map as the data for these algorithms. Now you can turn a great novel into a song, or create the symphony of your own smile. You can also buy your own hardware kits that let you turn any object into an electronic musical instrument. Who knew you could jam on a jelly doughnut?

THERE ARE SO MANY COOL THINGS I COULD DO!

I COULD ANIMATE MY COLLAGES, OR MAKE THEM INTERACTIVE, OR WRITE A PROGRAM WHERE THE COMPUTER GENERATES THEM FROM MY SELECTIONS!

Yup, you can do all those things. So we'd better start narrowing it down and come up with a plan.

Great brainstorming! And you have the beginnings of a really solid approach. Next, think about how you want the pieces to move and under what conditions. Then start writing out the idea in pseudocode.

I WANT TO USE A LOOP TO MAKE MY FACE SPIN IN A CIRCLE WHEN YOU CLICK IT!

```
if face_picture is clicked:
    rotate face_picture 360 degrees
```

MY COLLAGE HAS A PICTURE OF A PUPPY. I'M GOING TO HAVE THE PUPPY GET BIGGER AND BIGGER!

```
repeat forever:
    increase the width of the puppy_picture by 5px
    increase the height of the puppy_picture by 5px
```

Like all art, getting your code to work can take a little bit of experimentation and a whole lot of trial and error. But even when things don't go the way you planned, you can still come up with something amazing. Just ask Danielle Feinberg.

Danielle Feinberg

Finding Nemo, A Bug's Life, Monsters, Inc., WALL-E, Brave—Danielle Feinberg has put her coding knowledge to work in some of your favorite animated movies. Her job is an amazing blend of art and code. Here's what she has to say about how she got started, her favorite part of what she does, and how mistakes can lead to inspiration!

My title is Director of Photography for Lighting. I direct the lighting for our films. We build this three-dimensional world inside the computer and we have icons that represent lights that I move around in the world. So if it's sunset, I add a light that's the sun and put it near the horizon and color it orange and get nice purpley-blue light bouncing down from the sky. And I have control over the shadow, the color, the atmosphere, the quality of the light.

Danielle's work uses coding in all kinds of different ways.

The software we're using to place the lights is millions and millions of lines of code. Sometimes we write our own little bits of programming to make day-to-day life easier. Or we write code to create a new light. On *Finding Nemo* I did some work on a new light we had created called a Murk Light that mimics how light travels through the water.

Danielle's love of both coding and art goes all the way back to childhood, when she took her first coding class in the fourth grade.

My first programming experience was making pictures. Which totally fascinated me: you write this bit of code and you get a picture.

Both my parents are very artistic. My sister studied fine art in college, and from a very young age, my parents had us in art classes. We had this giant table in the basement, and it had any art supply you could want. My sister and I would go down there and spend hours and hours entertaining ourselves making art.

For Danielle, programming and creating art aren't that different.

Writing code is very much a creative process. I love this idea that you have a toolbox of commands with whatever language you're using. You a have certain goal that you're going after and you break it down into little pieces, but you have this finite number of commands that you can use. So it's quite creative figuring out, "How do I use this toolbox to get me there?"

Even when your ideas and code don't work out the way you plan, they can still lead you to creative inspiration, or something artists refer to as "happy accidents."

A lot of accidents in coding are not that happy. But very early on *Brave*, I was trying to create the look for the forest by putting some mist and lights into it. My code had a bug, and the computer completely dropped out all the lights so I was just left with the mist and everything else black. It gave depth to the forest and you got all these cool silhouettes of the plants. It was beautiful, and I never would have seen it if the computer hadn't barfed on the code to create that image. So it's important to be open to inspiration whenever it comes.

Staying open to opportunities and inspiration is an important part of being a successful programmer. But that's not all it takes. Staying open to other people's points of view has the power to turn a project into something that can actually change a life.

ROBOTS

SO WE'VE LOOKED AT GAMES, ART, AND DESIGN. WHAT KIND OF coding do you want to talk about next?

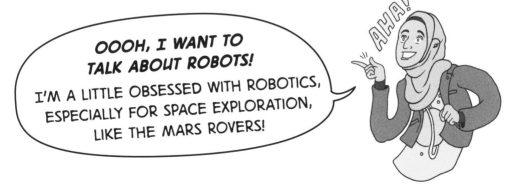

OOOH, I WANT TO TALK ABOUT ROBOTS!

I'M A LITTLE OBSESSED WITH ROBOTICS, ESPECIALLY FOR SPACE EXPLORATION, LIKE THE MARS ROVERS!

AHA!

I can't promise we'll be ready to make the next Mars rover by the end of this chapter, but there are tons of really useful coding projects involving robots.

These amazing machines have fueled our imaginations for centuries. When we talk about robots, most of you probably picture a humanoid droid with personality like something out of *Star Wars*—a mechanical human that can think, sense, respond, and move. But robots come in all different shapes and sizes. They also have a wide range of functions they can perform. And every single one of them relies on code to operate.

SO WHAT KINDS OF ROBOTS ARE OUT THERE RIGHT NOW? WHAT CAN THEY DO?

Robots help humans in all kinds of ways. There are robots designed to work in manufacturing, farming, and agriculture. These machines can be extremely helpful doing jobs that are tiring, dangerous, or too repetitive for people to want to do.

There are also robots being developed for health care, from robotic surgical tools to help doctors perform precision operations to robotic pill dispensers that follow nurses around hospitals dosing medicines. Engineers are also working on robotic doctors with screens and sensors that allow human doctors to communicate with and treat patients in remote areas.

Robotic limbs, prosthetics, and helper devices are changing the lives of people with disabilities and chronic illness, giving them back control of missing, damaged, or weakened body parts.

Then there are nanorobots. Though for now they are still the stuff of

science fiction, scientists and engineers are working hard to make these super tiny robots a reality. Nanorobots are designed to be much tinier than a grain of sand. We hope that one day these tiny robots could be able to enter the body to diagnose and treat disease without the need for invasive surgery. Engineers are also looking at how they can program nanorobots to function as swarms—much like insects—to work on a project or make repairs in hard-to-access environments.

Nanorobot
(magnified
×25 million!)

There are drones and remotely operated robots being used to navigate harsh and dangerous terrain—helping law enforcement, military personnel, and search and rescue teams operate in war zones and in the aftermath of natural disasters.

Scientists are using similar robots to explore places too far away or extreme for human survival. These robots are crawling over arctic ice caps, navigating the outer reaches of our solar system, and diving to the deepest depths of our oceans. The data they collect and images they send back are giving us a whole new perspective on our universe.

ocean-diving robot!

BUT THESE ARE ALL **BIG SUPER-ADVANCED ROBOTS** DOING AMAZING THINGS. HOW DO WE GET STARTED MAKING A ROBOT WE CAN USE IN OUR OWN LIVES?

Think about things you do every day. How could a robot help? And you don't have to think about robots that would help just you; your robot could also help others. Let's hear from Amber S., Emily D., Idaliz D., and Yananshalie S., four of our Girls Who Code who came up with a project to do just that.

Seeing Eye Bot

How did you come up with the idea for the Seeing Eye Bot?

AMBER: With Girls Who Code, we made a dancing robot. That was really fun, so when it was time to choose a project of our own, we wanted to do something with robots. But we didn't want to make it just dance—we wanted it to help people.

Tell us how it works.

YANANSHALIE: Its prototype uses a small robot that has motion and infrared sensors in the hardware, which can scan and detect objects in front of it, then calculate a path safely around the object. We programmed it to make different sounds when it approached the obstacle to communicate to the user where something is.

Did you get your robot to work?

YANANSHALIE: Yes, we got it to do the basics. It could navigate, see something, stop, go around. We built a maze out of boxes, and it could navigate through it.

What lessons did you take away from this project?

AMBER: The big question was how many sensors to give it. Next time, we would add more sensors; this version couldn't turn quite as much or find its way around stairs or ledges. But what's fun about building robots is that you can really see it working as you play around with it. You can test it as you build it, fix any issues, and edit things as they are happening.

What was your favorite part of this project?

YANANSHALIE: Collaborating was really helpful. We had four girls working on the project, and that's four different mind-sets. It made it easier to bounce ideas off each other and help each other on all the different aspects because everyone brought a different strength and point of view. And it was also fun.

So what do you think? Still want to build a space exploration robot, or do you have an idea for something that will be useful a little closer to home?

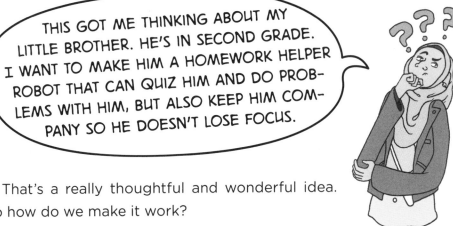

THIS GOT ME THINKING ABOUT MY LITTLE BROTHER. HE'S IN SECOND GRADE. I WANT TO MAKE HIM A HOMEWORK HELPER ROBOT THAT CAN QUIZ HIM AND DO PROBLEMS WITH HIM, BUT ALSO KEEP HIM COMPANY SO HE DOESN'T LOSE FOCUS.

That's a really thoughtful and wonderful idea. So how do we make it work?

WE'LL WANT TO PICK A RANDOM QUESTION AND HAVE THE ROBOT SAY IT!

from list of questions, pick one at random and save it in a variable
have robot say question text

AFTER THAT WE'LL HAVE THE ROBOT WAIT FOR A FEW SECONDS AND THEN SAY THE RIGHT ANSWER.

Wait five seconds
Have robot say question answer

Your little brother is going to be in for an incredible surprise. Take it from expert roboticist Ayanna Howard: there's nothing quite like the feeling of making your robot come to life.

Ayanna Howard

When it comes to robotics, Ayanna Howard has done it all. She's worked with NASA on robots that have gone to space. Her robots have explored the remote winter wastelands of the Antarctic. We got the chance to ask her about how she got interested in robots, what defines a robot, and how seeing things from a different perspective has informed her work.

I like robotics because you get direct feedback of whether your code is right or wrong. If you put in a wrong variable, your robot is going to hit the wall.

Robotics allows you to tap into all different learning styles. If I'm a visual learner, I see the robot moving. If I'm a tactile learner, I'm touching it, I'm moving it around and programming it. There's always that fear with computer science: "If I'm a programmer, am I gonna sit at a monitor all day?" In robotics you actually have to get up and interact.

Ayanna got her start working on robots for NASA, where she realized the value of seeing her work from the user's point of view.

I was looking at future Mars exploration missions. Even though it was space robotics and robotics for hazardous terrain, I focused on the reason why we want these robots in the first place: to do science. I needed to think about how scientists think, how they would navigate this terrain, and how they explore. Then when I came to Georgia Tech, the robots I

worked on there weren't going to space. I started doing research into the science of deploying robots in glacial environments and underwater so scientists can understand why the ice sheets are melting, what's going on with global warming. I got to work with climatologists, microbiologists, not just computer scientists.

Learning from the experiences of others is what led her to the work she is doing now.

I'm passionate about robotics in health care and for children with disabilities. I got started by chance. I was running a number of robotics camps, and one of my camps had a young lady who had a visual impairment and all our stuff was not accessible. She was really bright and made it work, and I just thought, *There is this whole demographic that I hadn't thought about in terms of access and leveling the playing field.* I started exploring that, interacting with kids with visual impairments and then kids with motor impairments.

Whatever the project, Ayanna always tries to remind her students of the value of their programming skills.

Coding is more than just 0's and 1's on the screen. When you create a piece of code that goes into a system at a hospital, you're saving lives. When you're creating a programming system that goes into an educational program, you are affecting generations of students. You have the power through your 0's and 1's to impact and change everything around you.

I'm excited to see how you girls will change the world by learning to code!

There's one more big topic to talk about. We use this type of code every day in a million different ways. In fact, you already hold the key to making these products better, and you probably don't even know it.

10

WEBSITES, MOBILE APPS, AND ONLINE SECURITY

SO HAVE YOU FIGURED OUT WHAT REALLY IMPORTANT AREA OF code we haven't talked about yet?

I'll give you a hint: it's something most of you use all the time. In fact, some of you are using it right now!

WEBSITES AND MOBILE APPS?

That's right! Website and mobile app design and development is one of the best ways to get your coding skills working for you right away. All you need is a computer and an idea, and you can dive right in and get creating. Teens and tweens are a giant market for apps and online services, and as a group you are already setting the trends. Not only are your likes and shares having a huge influence on which products are successful, but you're also the people teaching your parents about tech. This means that you have a huge say in what sites get visited and which apps get purchased, played, and promoted in your household. As a savvy tech user, you already know the products you like. So now you can get to work building them better!

Wow, you girls are totally on it. And that's exactly the point: as consumers of tech, you already know what you want and need. By learning to code, you don't have to wait for someone to come along and invent the perfect product for you—you can build it yourself!

Here are a couple of things to keep in mind when working on websites and apps.

WEBSITES

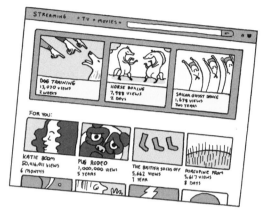

When it comes to websites, there are a lot of different ways to get started. You can use a ready-made template or code your own. Whatever you chose, one of the most important elements to think about when designing a website is the user experience (UX) design. What is the purpose of a site? Who will be using it? What information or services does it need to provide that user? These fundamental questions can help you decide which programing languages you should use to code your site and what features to give it.

Will your users be watching video clips and looking at portfolio pictures? How will those translate if they navigate using their phones? Will they be ordering merchandise or sending personal details? How do you make sure that information is kept private?

These questions are also important when designing apps. And there are a few other factors to consider as well.

APPS

There are several different kinds of apps. The differences between them are important because they affect how you code the apps.

NATIVE APPS: These come with a mobile device and live on its home screen. You access them through icons and can install new ones through an app store.

MOBILE WEB APPS: These are websites that look and act like apps, but are actually run through an internet browser. These apps are accessed through a website where you download the mobile version of the site. These apps can have limitations; for example, they can't always access the same hardware in your phone, like its camera or storage.

Apple and Android devices each have their own programming languages for apps. Androids use Android App Inventor or Java, and Apple's devices use Swift or Obj=C. It's worth thinking about how you want to distribute your app when it's done, so you know which language to choose from the get-go.

YOU MENTIONED KEEPING INFORMATION PRIVATE WHEN DESIGNING A WEBSITE. I'VE ALWAYS WONDERED ABOUT THAT. HOW DO WE MAKE SURE THE INFORMATION WE ARE PUTTING INTO OUR CODE, AND THE CODE ITSELF, STAYS SAFE?

Great question.

ONLINE SECURITY AND PRIVACY

As more and more of our lives go online, it is becoming increasingly important to protect our personal information, financial details, and even smart devices in our homes like thermostats and burglar alarms from malicious attacks. Unfortunately, there are hackers, criminals, and even hostile governments and political groups who can use weaknesses in CYBER SECURITY to steal identities and information, take money, and shut down services.

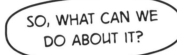

SO, WHAT CAN WE DO ABOUT IT?

There is a growing field of computer science that specializes in cyber security to fight this kind of crime. It operates in both in the commercial sector for companies and clients, and in the government sector for state and federal agencies. Specialties in this area include:

★ **DATA ENCRYPTION**—creating codes and passwords to keep data private.

★ **NETWORK MAINTENANCE**—working within a company to ensure their network is up to date, free from viruses and malicious software, and operating correctly.

★ **CYBER SECURITY TESTING AND DESIGN**—hacking networks to test them for security flaws and then designing solutions to fix the holes.

Data encryption and online security involve some pretty advanced coding, but here's how they apply to you right now. As you get started designing your app or website, always think carefully about what information you request from your users and how you are going to keep that safe. There are also lots of online resources to teach you programming best practices to keep your code and data secure.

I ALWAYS THOUGHT ONLINE SAFETY JUST MEANT US STAYING SAFE WHEN WE'RE ONLINE—LIKE NOT GIVING OUT OUR HOME ADDRESS TO STRANGERS OR CLICKING ON WEIRD LINKS THAT DOWNLOAD VIRUSES.

It's that, too. I'm sure the adults in your life have told you about some of the ways you need to use common sense when you are online—here are a couple of tips.

PERSONAL SAFETY ONLINE

As you've probably already discovered, the world can be a complicated place, especially for young women. The online world is no different. People there are just like people in everyday life. There are lots of people who want to help and connect, become friends, and form communities. But there are also people who mask their real identities in order to con, steal, bully, troll, and sometimes even harm vulnerable individuals. The digital world can give you incredible freedom to explore and connect, but online it's much harder to know whom you are actually connecting with than in the real world.

SMART, NOT SCARED

You don't have to be scared to be online, but you do have to be smart, especially with personal information. And anyone asking to meet up in person should be okay with meeting your family or guardians first. Period. If they are not, it's a big red flag, and you should tell a trusted adult. You'd never get in a car with a stranger on the street, right? So don't agree to meet up—or share personal information with—a stranger online, no matter how nice that person seems.

Members of our Seattle Girls Who Code community Celeste B., Julie P., Yasmin L., and Annie H. didn't like the idea of sitting around worrying about safety, so they built a really cool app called Guardian Angel to help empower young women to take charge of their personal safety.

Guardian Angel

How did you come up with the idea and what's the app all about?

JULIE: We knew we wanted to have something people could use and that would impact lives in a tangible way, not just purely entertaining. So we challenged ourselves to make something that would be of use on a day-to-day basis.

We knew there were a lot of safety apps on the market, but we didn't want something that would just contact someone or just track your location; we wanted to have a one-stop safety resource. And that was our vision for Guardian Angel.

So how's the app work? What can I do with it?

CELESTE: If you opened up the app, you would have the option to enable safety mode so it would have your location on. Then you have the option to hit an emergency button, and that will send a mass text with a Google map of your location to your safety contacts, a set group that you preprogram in the app. The app has its own database, and once it texts your location with the map, your safety contacts can get directions to where you are. Another feature uses Yelp to find open businesses so you can find a safe haven near you, then get directions from your location to the open business.

JULIE: We also have a page that would give you tips on staying safe and avoiding dangerous situations.

We wanted it to be usable for everyone, but we were thinking this would be particularly useful for people who are newly independent and aren't quite sure of themselves in busy cities or late at night.

Was this an app that you felt like you needed, or was it for someone else?

CELESTE: We all felt the need for this because we've all been in the situation of walking somewhere alone and it's creepy and you want to be watched over without someone hovering over you. And everyone we talked to in our class and outside felt there was a big need for this app.

JULIE: Our motto was: "Take safety back into your own hands," and we wanted to make sure the user can control who has access to what information at what time. You are always the one who's in control of what's going on around you. It wasn't just about "I'm feeling unsafe. I'm going to press this button and wait for someone to save me." It's about being the person who's doing something about a situation.

What was the process of building the app like? What language did you use?

CELESTE: None of us had programmed in Java or Swift, which is what you need to make an Android or Apple app. And we couldn't make a mobile web app because we needed to access the phone's text messages and contacts and geolocation. So we ended up using MIT App Inventor, which is a visual programming language that makes it easy to make Android apps.

JULIE: It's similar to Scratch, but for apps.

How did you like working together in a group?

JULIE: It was really cool because it was a constant collaborative effort. App Inventor wasn't the most intuitive program, so we had to channel our brainpower into one specific goal. We started to get into a really good flow, figuring out how to split up work and be collaborative at the same time.

So what do you think? Are you ready to start sketching out your apps?

I think our work here is done. This is what all the teachers, facilitators, mentors, partners, and members of the Girls Who Code community love to see: girls inspired, working together, creating, making, and writing code to improve lives and change the world.

This is exactly what Kaya Thomas has been doing ever since she learned to code in high school. She's proof of the power of coding to make good things happen.

Kaya Thomas

Kaya Thomas has loved reading ever since she was a kid, but she had a hard time relating to the characters in many of the books available in her library and local bookstore. So she decided to create an app to help kids find books and stories by people of color for people of color. Here's what she has to say about taking her app from big idea to reality.

When I was in high school, I would go to the library nearly every day and I was always reading a new book. I started to realize that none of the girls I was reading about had hair like me, skin like me, and it got really discouraging. I felt like, am I invisible? Why is my story not being told? Why can't I find these books? I really wished there was some type of resource, and that's where the idea stemmed from.

I always loved technology growing up and I've always been on social media. But I never imagined that I could create the things I love. That just never crossed my mind.

Then, when I was in college, I stumbled on computer science and fell in love with it. That's when I knew that I have the skills to bring this idea to life.

But it wasn't always easy for her.

I was excited about trying to be a computer science major. I got through a couple of intro courses, and then I got into one of the courses that was

pure mathematics. I didn't feel I had a strong math background, and I questioned if I could actually finish out the major. Luckily, the professor was encouraging and kept me motivated to stay. I didn't end up doing great in the class, but the fact that I was able to pass it was motivating. It showed me that I can do it, and I can't let myself get discouraged.

You'll feel moments of doubt, you'll feel moments of discouragement, but don't let those moments overcome you. Recognize that they're there, but then tell them to step aside so you can let your confidence shine through.

Realizing that knowledge, confidence, and determination are already there inside you is something Kaya tries to teach the students she mentors. For her, "giving back" is an important part of the work she's doing.

I want to share my experiences and insights and say, "You can rise above me. You can be more successful than me." It's our job, if we're going to be in the tech industry, to make this a space for more women, more people of color, more people of every walk of life to come in and be able to innovate with us and solve problems that are affecting their communities. And the only way to do that is to reach the younger ones who are going to come after us and say, "We're here to support you. You can create more than us, you can do better than we did."

CONCLUSION

YOU MADE IT! WE'RE AT THE END OF THE BOOK, BUT FOR YOU, IT'S just the beginning. If we've done our job right, you are ready to go out and start coding. There's a whole world of creation, invention, and inspiration just waiting for you.

SO WHAT NOW?

If you are ready to start coding, the first thing you can do is visit our website: GirlsWhoCode.com. We've put together all kinds of resources to help you take the next step in your coding adventure. And of course, we can give you all the information you need to find or start a Girls Who Code club near you. Once you join a club, you'll become part of a community of other girls learning to code in your area and across the country.

As you get older, once you get to high school and start preparing for college, our community can offer advice on choosing computer science classes and college prep to help you declare a CS major or minor. When

you're ready for college, we want to connect you with schools, graduate programs, and, ultimately, companies that will lead you to a fulfilling career in tech and tech-related fields.

Because those careers are out there waiting for you. Take it from my friend Debra Sterling, a successful engineer and entrepreneur. She created GoldieBlox—building blocks for girls—and is busy growing her company. Even so, she's still taking time to learn to code.

> DEBRA: I studied mechanical engineering and product design, and I took a couple CS classes. But one of my biggest regrets is not taking more CS in college. So I just recently started teaching myself to code. I think kids should be learning CS at the same time they learn to read and write. Having those skills and understanding the way the world works is going to be critical to build this world and make it a better place for all of us to live.

Still not sure if coding's for you? I'll leave it to the experts to tell you what they think.

Julie and Celeste from Guardian Angel:

JULIE: Try it. Just take a course. You can't knock it until you try it because there's sooo much you can do with it. I think a lot of people have a hesitation because they have an image of people sitting at a laptop for twenty hours, but it's so totally not. It's not just a skill; for a lot of people it becomes a passion.
CELESTE: It can be applied in any field. You can enhance whatever you're interested in with computer science.

Tran from LED It Glow:

I know there are people who hear "computer science and coding" and are like, "Eeewww." But try it. I didn't think I would like it, but then once I started, I really loved it, and it changed my whole career path. I definitely want to keep going with computer science.

Glory and Zahraa from Career Couture:

GLORY: Almost everything you do has something to do with coding. And you can combine it with almost everything—fashion and empowerment, or media or anything else.
ZAHRAA: I didn't think I was going to become a Girl Who Codes. I didn't think I was smart enough to put together simple algorithms. I think a lot of girls don't want to do it because they doubt themselves, and my advice is: believe in yourself, because you can change the world, one line of code at a time.

That's what I'm here to tell you.

YOU LEARNING TO CODE MATTERS BECAUSE YOU MATTER.
Your voice, your point of view, your creative ideas and energy matter. Women make up 50 percent of the world's population. We are half of the people on this planet! So how come we aren't half of the CEOs of Fortune 500 companies or entrepreneurs? Why aren't we half of the world's leaders and politicians? Why aren't we half of the world's inventors and change makers?

We are; we just haven't had the opportunity to show it yet. By mastering technology that is essential to the jobs and industries of the future, we can make it happen. You are brave, you are strong, you are smart, you are a Girl Who Codes. And you can change the world.

GLOSSARY

ALGORITHM

An algorithm is a set of steps that a computer follows to complete a task. You can write algorithms that do all kinds of things, from solving math problems to writing music! (*see* algorithmic composition)

ALGORITHMIC COMPOSITION

Algorithmic composition means using algorithms, or step-by-step lists of instructions, to create music with computers. Imagine a symphony written entirely by robots!

API

An API, or application programming interface, is a set of rules that lets applications talk to each other. For example, instead of coding your own map from scratch, you can use the Google Maps API to include a Google map on your site or app.

APPLICATION

An application is a software program that runs on your computer, on the web, or on smaller devices like a smart phone or tablet. Web applications, like social media sites or calendars, are different from websites because they don't just present information— they need input from people to work. There are applications for everything, from word processing and games to editing photos and connecting with friends on social media.

APPLICATION FLOW

An application flow, or "flow chart," is a way of using pictures and arrows to show what will happen in your application and the order in which things will occur. Mapping out the application flow can help you work through the logical steps to make your program run.

BINARY

A binary code translates words or computer processor instructions into a series of 1's and 0's that tell computers what to do. In binary code, the word "hi" is 01101000 01101001.

BINARY NUMBER

A binary number is a normal number that has been translated into a code of 1's and 0's. In the binary system, each digit of a number is called a **bit**.

BOOLEANS

In coding, Booleans are true or false questions that help your computer know what to do as it works through your code. Booleans are used in "if" statements, where if the statement is true then something will happen, but if the statement is false then something different will happen.

BRAINSTORMING

Brainstorming is a way of working as a group to think up creative solutions to big problems. In a brainstorming session, there are no bad ideas!

CODE

Code is what people use to describe the steps a computer program should take. Code lets us write instructions in our own words that the computer can understand.

COLLABORATION

Collaboration is when two or more people work together on a project or task. Online collaboration tools like GitHub make it possible for coders in different parts of the country to work on the same code all at the same time.

COMPILER

When you write code, you use words in ordinary language to tell the computer what to do. A compiler is like a translator that takes the words you write and translates them into "machine code" that the computer can understand.

COMPUTATIONAL THINKING

Computational thinking helps us work logically through big problems by breaking them down into smaller pieces, looking for patterns, and then using this information to come up with a step-by-step solution.

COMPUTER CODING/COMPUTER PROGRAMMING

When you write code or program a computer, you're telling a computer what to do. Even though they seem smart, computers actually can't do anything without code written by people!

COMPUTER SCIENCE

Computer science (or CS for short) is the study of computers and the different ways they can be used. Computer scientists write programs that do all sorts of things, from solving complicated medical problems to creating music and art.

CONDITIONAL

A conditional is an element of code that only happens if something else happens. Conditionals are also called "if" statements, because "if" something happens, then something else will happen.

CORE4

Core4 computer science concepts is a phrase invented by Girls Who Code that refers to what we consider the four core concepts of computer science—variables, loops, conditions, and functions—that exist across nearly all programming languages.

CYBER SECURITY

Cyber security means protecting the data on your computer, phone, or other devices from being stolen or damaged.

D.R.Y. (DON'T REPEAT YOURSELF)

D.R.Y, or "Don't Repeat Yourself," means not writing the same code over and over again, so that it's easier to read and edit. If you want to do something more than once, you can write a function or use a loop instead.

DATA

Data is any information that you put into a computer to get it to perform a task or make a calculation.

DEBUGGING

Code rarely works the first time. Debugging is finding out why your code is not working and fixing the problems. Debugging got its name when Grace Hopper found a moth in her computer (an actual bug!) that was making the computer malfunction.

DESIGN

A design is a plan, either written or drawn, that gives instructions for how something should look and function. For example, a design for a dress tells you how that dress should be made, and a design for an iPhone app will show how that app will work. The people who create these plans are **designers**.

DESIGN-BUILD-TEST CYCLE

In the design-build-test cycle, you design something, build it so that it works, test it out, and then use what you've learned to make the design better. Since it's a cycle, you keep doing it until you're happy with what you've made.

DIGITAL ART AND DESIGN

Digital art and design bring technology into the process of creating art and designs, from editing photos to using code to lighting a scene in an animated movie.

DOCUMENTATION

Documentation is the information that describes a website or app to its users. Most documentation is online these days, but some examples of old-school documentation are paper owner's manuals or help guides.

EFFICIENCY

In computer science, efficiency measures how much you get out of a computer program compared with how much you put into it. Very efficient computer programs can process data quickly without using much computer memory—a lot like how a cheetah can run fast without using much energy.

FEATURE CREEP

Feature creep is the addition of extra elements, or features, to a project even though users might not really need them. Those features "creep" in, making your project more complicated than it needs to be.

FUNCTION

A function is a list of steps in a program that are all wrapped up together, like a math problem. When you give information, or "input" to the function, it processes that information and gives you back an answer, or an "output."

GENERATIVE ART

Generative art is art that has been made, at least partly, using computers. If you wanted to code a character's hair in an animation, for example, you could either code every single hair or use code to duplicate the hairs realistically and save yourself some time. The animators who created Princess Merida in the Pixar movie *Brave* used generative art to give her a full head of hair that moves and behaves the way curly hair does in real life without having to animate every individual strand.

GENRE

A video game genre is a group of games that have similar challenges. For example, educational games would be grouped together in one genre, while adventure games would be grouped in another.

HARDWARE

Hardware refers to the physical pieces that make up a computer or device, like keyboards, monitors, and memory cards.

HELLO, WORLD

"Hello, world" is a simple computer program that tells your computer to say "Hello, world!" This is one of the first programs people run when they're learning a new programming language.

INPUT

The information and instructions that you give to a computer are called "input." When you type on a keyboard or use your fingerprint to unlock your phone, you're giving the computer input about what you want it to do.

INTEGRATED DEVELOPMENT ENVIRONMENT (IDE)

An IDE, or integrated development environment, is an application that coders use to make computer programs. IDEs bring a few different tools, like compilers and debuggers, into one program that helps developers write software more easily.

LIBRARY

A library is a collection of resources that you can use in your code. You can use the same library in many different programs, which helps you avoid having to write out the same thing over and over again.

LOGIC

An organized way of thinking that makes sense to a computer.

LOGIC ERROR

A logic error is a bug in a program's code that makes it work differently than it should. For example, an "if" statement might evaluate to false when it should actually be true.

LOOP

A loop is a way of writing one piece of code that repeats multiple times. If I want to draw a square, I can write one loop that says "go straight, then turn right" and have it repeat four times instead of writing eight lines of code.

OUTPUT

Output is how a computer behaves based on a combination of your input and the code of the program. So, when you use your finger to tap on an app icon (input), the application opens (output)!

PARAMETER

A parameter is a kind of variable that gets passed through a function. For example, in the function "def f(x): . . . ," the "x" is the parameter. The words *parameter* and *argument* are sometimes used to mean the same thing.

PROCESS (NOUN)

A process is a program that is running on your computer or device. One application can have a few different processes all running at the same time!

PROGRAMMING LANGUAGE

A programming language is a set of rules and instructions used to write computer programs. There are many different programming languages that you can use to do different things.

PSEUDOCODE

Pseudocode is a description of code that is easily readable by humans but not computers. Pseudocode is used to record the logic of your code before you translate it into code that computers will understand.

ROBOTICS

Robotics is a branch of computer science that deals with building machines that use code to complete tasks. Robots are being built every day to do amazing things, from assisting doctors to exploring the bottom of the ocean.

SOFTWARE

Software means anything that can be stored electronically, like programs or instructions. All software falls into one of two categories: **systems software** is the operating system that makes your computer work, while **applications software** means any kind of program that you can use to do work, like a photo editor or a word processor.

STORYBOARD

A storyboards is like a comic that you can draw to map out what will happen in your program or game. Some storyboards might look fancy, but they don't need to be. Even simple stick figures can help you figure out how your program or game should play out!

STRING

A string is a data type made up of characters that can include letters, spaces, and numbers. You can usually tell something is a string if it's in quotation marks—even numbers can be strings! Some examples of strings are "girlswhocode" and "girls who code" and "12345."

SYNTAX

Syntax is the order of letters, numbers, and symbols in code—a lot like writing sentences in English! Proper syntax is important for keeping your program happy and working. Syntax is the difference between, "Hello meet! You, nice it's to" and "Hello, it's nice to meet you!"

SYNTAX ERROR

A syntax error happens when the syntax of your code isn't quite right—something isn't where it should be. Sometimes, an error as tiny as a semicolon (;) in the wrong place can make a big difference!

TEXT EDITOR

An application that can be used to compose text, including computer code. Many text editors are made specifically for coding and include features like quick shortcuts and automatic error detection.

USER EXPERIENCE (UX)

User experience (UX) is the experience that people have when using a product, from mobile apps to microwaves. A well-designed UX makes a product easy and fun to use without the user needing to be taught how to use it. Good UX is the reason toddlers can use tablets!

VARIABLES

Variables are like containers that are used in a program to store and remember information. Variables can hold numbers, strings of letters, and even whether something is true or false!

VIDEO GAME DEVELOPMENT

Video game development is the process of coming up with and creating a video game! Girls Who Code students have made amazing games that address important topics, like endangered species and social issues.

VISUALIZATION

Visualization means using computers to make images, graphics, or animations that help you tell stories with data. If you've ever seen an interactive map or an infographic, then you've seen visualizations!

WEBSITE

A website is a place on the web that presents information to the public but does not require interaction from people. Websites are a lot like school assemblies, where a speaker comes and talks to you about something, but you don't really talk back. You can make an awesome website with just a little HTML and CSS knowledge!

WIREFRAME

A wireframe is a way of planning the structure and function of a website or application using simple boxes and lines. Each wireframe is like a puzzle that tells you what will go where, and how all the pieces will fit together.

Acknowledgments

For the past five years, I've seen tens of thousands of girls from every state and city learn how to code and build products that are solving our most urgent problems: gun violence, climate change, cancer, poverty. This book is for them, and for the countless others who, like me, are inspired by them. It's a call to arms to girls across the country and the world to learn to code so they too can be change makers.

I want to thank Sarah Hutt for translating the complex world of coding into language that we all can understand. You immersed yourself in the Girls Who Code community, and we won't let you leave too quickly.

Thank you to Jeff Stern for his incredible work on this book. I approached him about working on this project almost three years ago and he immediately said yes. An excellent teacher and a creative person, he would, I knew, be able to make basic computer science principles fun and interesting.

Thank you to the entire Girls Who Code team, especially those who contributed to this project: the ultimate girl who codes, Emily Reid, as well as Charlotte Stone, Chrissy Ziccarelli, Claire Cook, Deborah Singer, Ellen McCullagh, Eric Gunther, Hanna Gully, Huda Qureshi, Jessamine Bartley-Matthews, Leah Gilliam, and Sarah Judd.

Thank you, Richard Pine, my incredible agent, who had a larger vision for this than I could've imagined. His amazing team at Inkwell was a privilege to work with, including Eliza Rothstein and Nathaniel Jacks.

Thank you, Andrea Tsurimi, our illustrator, whose imaginative drawings brought our characters and their stories to life.

Thank you, Kendra Levin, a rock star editor, for your expertise and leadership. You made this book a reality. I also want to thank Kate Renner, our art director, and Bethany Bryan, our copyeditor.

I want to thank the entire team at Viking, particularly Ken Wright. We're so excited to collaborate with the Penguin Young Readers Group marketing team and sales force to bring this book to girls across the world.

Thank you to all of the inspiring women who shared their stories for this book: Dona Bailey, Ayanna Howard, Chelsea Howe, Danielle Feinberg, Debra Sterling, and Kaya Thomas.

Thank you to Amber S., Annie H., Celeste B., Emily D., Faith W., Glory K., Idaliz D., Julie P., Kenisha J., Maria M., Nany N., Serena V., Yananshalie S., Yasmin L., and Zahraa L. for letting us feature your projects.

And a million thanks to the many more Girls Who Code students and budding young coders whose colorful stories and feedback helped shape the book you're now holding.

INDEX

in video game development, 115

Core4 computer science concepts,
    38–39, 48

cyber security, 145–47

data
    definition of, 34
    encryption of, 145, 146
data visualization, 123
debugging errors, 95–105
    and embracing imperfection, 104–5
    finding the error, 98
    getting help with, 98–101
    with integrated development
        environments, 103
    with print function, 102–3
    by reading code, 102
    taking breaks from, 103–4
    talking about, 101–2
    term, 96
    and types of errors, 96–97
design, 64–71
    considering time requirements, 67
    and cyber security, 150–51
    establishing a need for product, 64–65
    establishing the demand for product, 66
    and feature creep, 70–71
    researching similar products, 65
    and user experience, 68, 143
    visualizing the product, 68–70
design and fashion, 124

design-build-test cycle, 59–60

designers, 68

digital art and design, 119–29
    brainstorming for, 126–27
    in data visualization, 123
    in design and fashion, 124
    and LED It Glow display, 120–22
    in music, 124–25
    tips from a pro developer, 128–29
    in visual art, 122–23
discouragement, dealing with, 153

divide by zero errors, 97

drones, 133

D.R.Y. (Don't Repeat Yourself), 47

Eckert, J. Presper, 22

education options for girls who code,
    154–55

Electronic Numerical Integrator and
    Computer (ENIAC), 22, 23

"else" statements, 37–38, 45

employment opportunities in
    computing, 5

equal signs with "if" statements, errors
    relating to, 97

errors: *See* debugging errors

Feinberg, Danielle, 127, 128–29

Forecast Fabulous app, 53–55

friends
    collaborating with, 63
    and debugging questions, 100